Wholistic Witchcraft

Magick for the mind, body and soul

Reader Reviews

Jennifer Faulkner

This beautiful book offers a glimpse into the author's life as a witch in modern society. We see how witchcraft can be drawn upon to heal, to create, to divine and to guide us through difficulties many of us face, such as dealing with difficult people, living in harmony and setting up sacred spaces wherever we are in the world.

As the author guides us through the building blocks of a heartfelt and respectful practice, she takes us on a practical journey of discovering and honing our individual craft. It is both a handy sourcebook and an experiential journey, inviting us to cultivate progressively deepening layers of personal magickal insights.

It is a timely reminder of what many have forgotten about working with the cycles, the seasons and the magick that exists all around us.

Bev Neumann

I have been a practising witch for many years and am still learning lots. Bella's book has great guidance, and is an easy read and even easier to follow – with a few giggles too – for anyone who is starting on their magickal path.

I have been feeling a little disconnected from my path lately but after reading Bella's book I am feeling more connected than ever. I have a fire burning inside me that has inspired me to fall deeper into my path.

Bella is a great mentor and I will be highly recommending her book.

Barbara Trainor

The magick of *Wholistic Witchcraft* is that the authenticity of the author shines through. Within these pages you will find practical everyday information and examples to help bring your own personal magick to life.

Sarah Lockyer

Wholistic Witchcraft is a beautifully written book. The flow of the subject matter helps guide the reader through a wealth of information without feeling overwhelmed. Readers are taken on a journey of knowledge, self-analysis and self-discovery before stepping into their power. The activities and rituals found at the end of each chapter make it easy for the reader to incorporate wholistic witchcraft into day-to-day life and use what they have learnt in a practical way.

The book is suited to people of all abilities and backgrounds, and Bella's eclectic style and years of practical knowledge show in her writing. Beginners will find the book to be a great learning tool, with the tasks, information and ritual layouts being easy to understand and follow. The more advanced witches will benefit greatly as the practical tasks help to overcome magickal blockages or burnout by slowly integrating magick into every aspect of the reader's life. It is also a great reference book when creating your own magickal workings.

Wholistic Witchcraft is truly for the mind, body and spirit.

For my brother, an old soul who was wise well beyond his years. It was he who inspired me to follow this path, and I am grateful to him for this beautiful legacy every day.

Wholistic Witchcraft

Magick for the mind, body and soul

Belinda Payne

Wholistic Witchcraft: Magick for the mind, body and soul
Belinda Payne
© Belinda Payne 2020

bella@wiccid.com.au
www.wiccid.com.au

This book is sold with the understanding that the author is not offering specific personal advice to the reader. For professional advice, seek the services of a suitable, qualified practitioner. The author disclaims any responsibility for liability, loss or risk, personal or otherwise, that happens as a consequence of the use and application of any of the contents of this book.

All rights reserved. This book may not be reproduced in whole or part, stored, posted on the internet, or transmitted in any form or by any means, electronic, mechanical, photocopying, recording, or other, without permission from the author of this book.

Editing, design and publishing support by www.AuthorSupportServices.com

Section header illustrations by Catherine Joy

ISBN: 978-1-922375-00-1

A catalogue record for this book is available from the National Library of Australia

Foreword

Hello, dear heart.

I'm honoured to be writing this foreword for my dear friend, Bella.

As the owner of one of the largest ranges of online spirituality and witchcraft supplies in Australia, The Sacred Willow, I know people are seeking more magick in their lives. Magick is the innate power within all of us, and more and more people want to access their own magickal power with guidance and direction they can trust. They want real connections, honesty, integrity and a more wholistic way of living.

This book seeks to provide that connection by empowering readers to live a wholistic life, in tune with their mind, body and soul.

I've had the privilege of meeting a lot of Pagans during my own journey. They were real, down-to-earth people who practised what they preached and lived their lives connected to the world in a tangible, magickal way.

And when I first met Bella, it was clear to me that she was one of these genuine people.

Over the past few years, I've attended several of Bella's circles. I can honestly say that she's a Witch who lives her beliefs and helps others to live as the best version of themselves as well. I've watched her inspire people and help them on their Pagan journey by sharing the knowledge she's gained over 25 years as a practising Witch.

The circles Bella runs are inspiring, well-thought-out spaces that allow women and girls to explore their own power and creativity. Her weekend retreats and workshops encourage deeper exploration of Self and connection to each other, Spirit and Nature.

And her Wiccid Academy has taught many Witches more advanced levels of magick. Time and time again, Bella has shifted me into another way of thinking and helped me and many others to connect with our own power.

This book is all about wholistic living, which I think is one of the most important things we can achieve in life. When we're in tune with Nature, ourselves and those around us, we live a much more beautiful and fulfilling life. We tread more lightly on the Earth, which is more important now than ever.

Through the journey, rituals, reflection questions and information in this book, Bella provides you with a framework to step into your power and incorporate magick into your life. She explores the connection between witchcraft and wholistic living: a vital connection that helps to increase your energy and, in turn, your abilities.

But she goes beyond simply providing you with the keys to a more healthy and fulfilled life. She also gives you tools to deepen your connection to your own power and create a magickal life that works for you.

My wish for you is that you take this book and use it to become the most magickal version of yourself that you can be. Be brave, dear heart. Step onto the path within this book, find that spark of magick within you and live your best wholistic, magickal life.

Bless x

Courtney Stark
Owner ~ The Sacred Willow
www.thesacredwillow.com.au

Contents

Introduction: Merry Meet!   1

Section 1
And so the Journey Begins...

Chapter 1: Preparing for Your Journey   11

Chapter 2: Energy Work   29

Chapter 3: Cycles   45

Chapter 4: Elemental Magick   73

Chapter 5: Deities and Magickal Beings   89

Section 2
Tools to Aid Your Journey

Chapter 6: Divination   109

Chapter 7: Sacred Spaces   125

Chapter 8: Keeping Your Magick with You   143

Chapter 9: Your Circle   155

Section 3
Spiralling Into Transformation

Chapter 10: Healing	177
Chapter 11: Love Thyself	197
Chapter 12: Journey to Shadow	209
Chapter 13: Reclaiming Your Power	223
Conclusion	233
Yearning to Go Deeper?	239
Acknowledgements	245

Appendices

Appendix A: Sabbats	249
Appendix B: Colours	253
Appendix C: Crystals	259
Appendix D: Gods and Goddesses	267
Appendix E: Tools	271
Appendix F: Animals	273
Appendix G: Herbs, Spices and Resins	277
Appendix H: Flowers	281
Appendix I: Recommended Resources	285
References	287

INTRODUCTION

Merry Meet!

Welcome to your journey into wholistic witchcraft

Merry meet to you, dear reader. I'm Belinda, known as Bella amongst my magickal friends. Thank you for joining me on this magickal journey. If you've picked up this book, chances are that you have an interest in either wholistic living or witchcraft, or both.

What is wholistic witchcraft?

I define 'wholistic witchcraft' as living wholistically while also travelling your magickal path. This means living with your mind, body and soul in alignment, and nurturing yourself physically, mentally and spiritually on a daily basis. This is not only vital for your total wellbeing, but also for your witchcraft.

Without that foundation, you won't be able to keep your vibration – AKA your energy – high. And only when you're vibrating at that high level can you perform your best magick.

How I discovered wholistic witchcraft

My journey with witchcraft began over 25 years ago. My journey with a wholistic lifestyle, on the other hand, began about five years later, when I became horribly ill with Graves' disease – a thyroid disorder.

At the time, as well as being a practising Wiccan, I was into organic food and natural medicine – but I wouldn't say I was living an overall 'wholesome' lifestyle. Like so many people, I was quite fond of burning the candle at both ends and often got run down.

Having this disease affected my mental clarity, weight, overall health and confidence. So, over the 18+ years that followed, I tried a million diets, eating plans, healing techniques, supplements, doctors and detoxes.

The only thing that remained constant for me over all these years was my spirituality – my magick. And after a while, I started to bring my knowledge of both magick and wholistic health and living together.

My journey started with discovering the five keys to a wholistic lifestyle

In addition to all the symptoms I've mentioned above, the disease also affected my magick. That was mostly because of its effects on my energy levels. Some days, my energy was high, while on others, it was low again.

So, over time, my mission became to find a way to even my energy levels out. And eventually, I found that that there were five keys that kept me functioning at my best:

- good nutrition
- adequate sleep
- lots of water
- daily movement
- activities that nurtured my soul.

You'll read more about each of these keys and why they're so important in Chapter 1. I'll also remind you every now and then throughout the book to check in with yourself to see how you're tracking with each of them.

Introduction: Merry Meet!

Now, why do I focus on these keys in a book about magick? Because I believe that living by these keys can improve anyone's health and that better health will then inevitably raise your vibration – all the better for your magick ♥.

Only then could I add in the foundations of magick

A wholistic magickal lifestyle goes far beyond just focusing on those five keys, however. That's why this book starts there but then provides you with the information and tools to explore and define your own magickal path.

So once you've started to work on the five keys, you'll be ready to discover:

- **The basics you'll need to step out onto the path:** You'll learn all about energy, cycles, elements, deities and other magickal beings, and how to work with each of these in the first section of this book.
- **Tools to help you on your way:** Then, in the second section, you'll discover tools that can help you to explore and grow spiritually – divination, creating sacred spaces, ways to keep your magick with you, and building a supportive community around you.
- **Advanced techniques to help you spiral into transformation:** Finally, in the third section, we'll start to explore deeper with higher-level techniques that include healing, self-love, shadow work and reclaiming your power.

The aim is to start with the basic (but essential) foundations and gradually move, step-by-step, along your path to true self-discovery and wholistic living. Eventually, if you're willing to put in the work, you'll evolve to a place where your mind, body, soul and magick are flowing harmoniously together in a beautiful dance of life.

Wholistic Witchcraft

The journey of the witchling

To help you understand how all these elements work together, I'll ask you to imagine your journey through this book as the journey of the Fool in the Tarot. Here, however, I'll call the Fool 'the witchling' instead.

Imagine the witchling having been sheltered in a cave all her life. Every now and then, she looks outside from the entrance, longing to discover what the world out there is really like.

Finally, one day, she takes her brave first step outside of the cave. And so begins a journey of learning, discovery, challenges, triumphs, facing fears, evolution and, ultimately, stepping into her power.

Along the way, the witchling discovers that she's had everything she ever needed inside her all along. That's what my goal of this book is for you, dear reader. I want you to discover and reawaken the magick that's already inside you.

How to use this book

I designed this book as a journey, so I strongly recommend reading and working through it at least once from start to finish.

After that, you may want to come back and reread specific sections or chapters later on as they become relevant again in your life. If so, that's totally OK. But, in the same way that we all need to walk before

Introduction: Merry Meet!

we can run, I don't recommend skipping straight to the advanced techniques.

Plus, in order to get the most out of this book, you need to actually *experience* as much of this journey as possible. It's not enough to just read and take in the words.

That's why, in each chapter, I've included a ritual that will help you to integrate these teachings and propel you forward. I highly recommend performing the ritual at the end of each chapter before you go on to the next. The process of experiencing your magick will help you to bring together everything you've learnt and help you to understand the teachings more fully.

Then, after each ritual, you'll find suggestions for integrating everything you've learnt into your wholistic lifestyle. Again, I'd suggest trying to put some of these into practice before you move on to the next chapter – for exactly the same reasons I mentioned above.

Finally, at the end of each chapter you'll find a set of questions for you to explore and ponder. I recommend using a journal to record any answers, feelings or findings. I'll also prompt you to record anything magickal you've learnt or observed in your Book of Shadows (more about this book in Chapter 1).

Dearest reader, I hope that within these pages, you find wisdom and inspiration in your quest for good health, a peaceful mind and a deeper understanding of magick.

Many blessings, and I look forward to guiding you on your journey,

Bella x

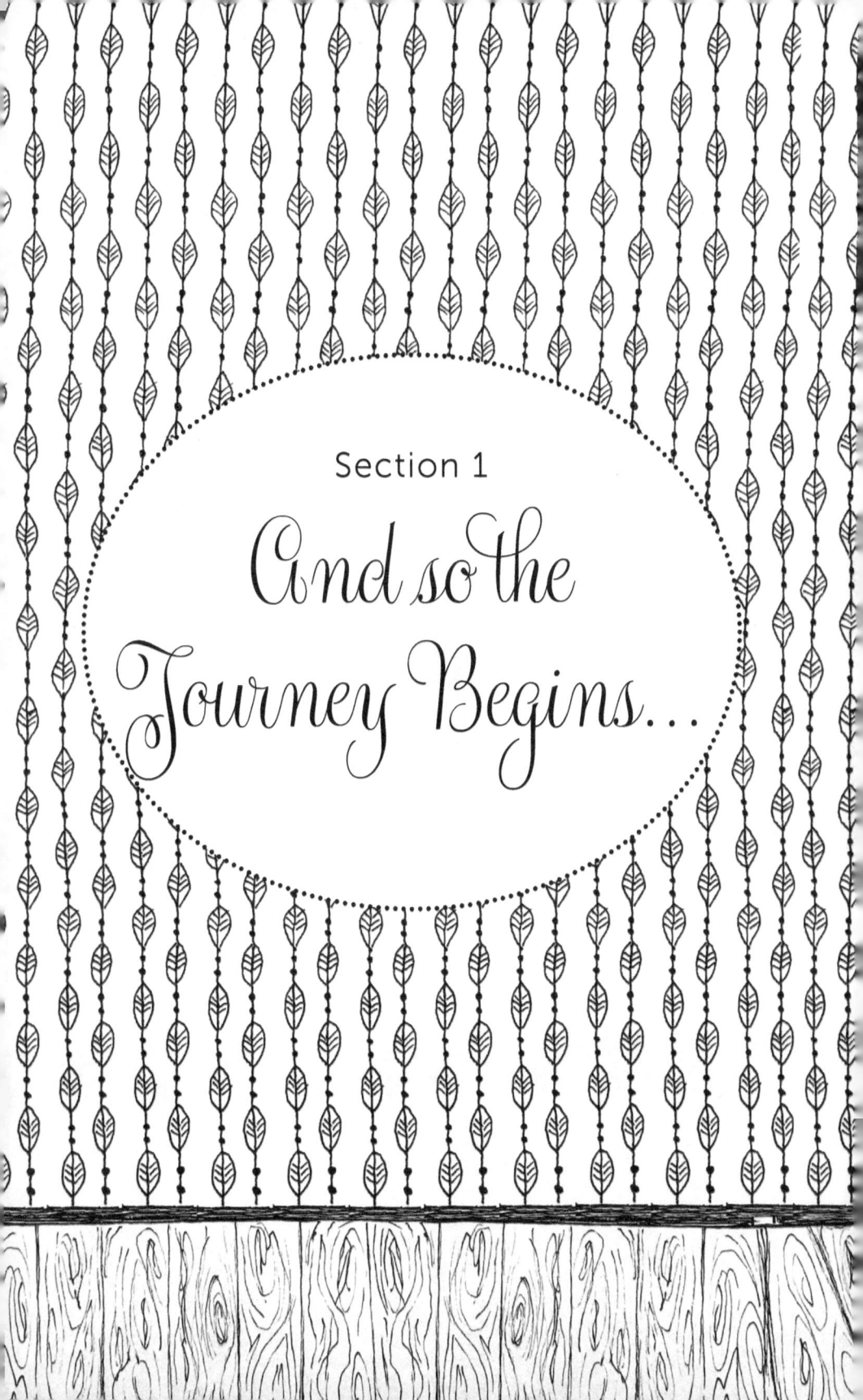

Section 1

And so the Journey Begins…

The witchling emerges from her cave and is instantly exposed to the magick of the elements. She feels the energy of the Earth beneath her feet, and the breeze whispers around her body. The heat of the Sun shines on her face, and she senses the flow of the water nearby.

As she travels her path, she feels the strength of the natural energies around her. Entranced, she begins to understand how they work together and how they seem to affect her. She notices with delight new buds on the trees, flowers on the brink of blooming and mothers with their babes taking advantage of Nature's abundance. Everything coexists gracefully as if it's all one.

As the day turns to night, the witchling notices the journey of the Moon and Sun. She begins to appreciate how the energies of each are so different, yet so essential to not only each other but also to life itself.

As she journeys further on her magickal path, she begins to feel into what the Divine is. She understands how it is alive in everything — and she comes to know that everything, including herself, is connected.

Greetings, dear reader. Welcome to the first section of this book and the first steps of your journey to a magickal wholistic life. These chapters will give you the basic tools you need to get started on your quest. As you travel through this section, you'll discover what you need to do to prepare for and start learning about the foundations of both magickal and wholistic living.

These foundations include:

- what wholistic living is (Chapter 1)
- how energy works (Chapter 2)
- what cycles are – both Nature's and our own (Chapter 3)
- how to connect with the elements of Nature (Chapter 4)
- what it means to work with deities (Chapter 5).

It's really important to understand these foundations before you continue on to the deeper, more complex work in Sections 2 and 3. It's very difficult to successfully perform a spell if you don't know how to work with the influence of the Moon, for example. And it's just as hard if you don't understand how the energies you're connecting with will work to manifest your intention.

To truly understand these foundational elements, you need practical experience to help the wisdom you learn sink into your bones. That's why, as I mentioned in the introduction, each chapter includes practical tasks and rituals to perform. I can tell you honestly that my own understanding and knowledge exploded once I started putting what I'd read into practice.

It's a magickal thing!

Finally, by the time you finish this section, you'll know how to do a ritual (if you don't already). You'll also truly understand what it means to wholistically care for your mind, body and soul.

May you stay present and aware as you enjoy this journey,

Bella x

CHAPTER 1

Preparing for Your Journey

Let this magickal journey begin!

As the title suggests, this book is a journey that flows beautifully along a path to transformation. As you take it, you'll discover wisdom, advice, tools and guidance.

Preparing is essential for any successful journey, so in this chapter, you'll find a list of the basic items you'll need to begin. However, it's not enough to just have the tools – you also need to ensure you set aside the time and space to learn to use them. That's why this chapter also contains:

> Preparing is essential for any successful journey.

- tips to organise your time so you can integrate what you learn into your daily life
- an awareness exercise to help you begin with clarity
- your first ritual, which will help you to clear space in your schedule if organising your time is a little difficult.

Good preparation will help to ensure your journey flows with ease and grace, and allow you to immerse yourself in the teachings.

One small step is all it will take you to begin, and I'll be here with you all the way.

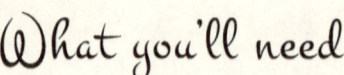

What you'll need

You won't need to buy a heap of expensive items to get started, but I'd recommend at least having the following:

- **Two journals of any kind.** You'll use one to record your answers to questions at the end of each chapter, plus any insights, thoughts and observations that come to you along the way. The other will become your Book of Shadows (see below).

- **A smudge stick, cleansing spray or palo santo stick.** At first, you'll use this mostly to cleanse yourself and your sacred space before a ritual. Later on, however, you'll also use it to clear negative energy in your home and raise your own vibration (energy) whenever needed.

  You only need one of them, not all three (unless you want them all!), and you can easily buy them at new age stores or online. I use eBay or Australian online suppliers. Please see Appendix I or check Google to find stockists that are best suited or closest to you.

- **Red and green candles (one of each), and a supply of white tealights.** You'll use the red candle to represent the God, while the green one will represent the Goddess. You'll need these for rituals and for when you create sacred spaces.

Creating your Book of Shadows

A Book of Shadows is a journal that you use to record magickal information, rituals and the wisdom you've gained from the rituals you've performed. It's a sacred book that's completely personal to you.

That means it can be a fancy book you find at a bookstore or online, or a simple blank-page visual diary. You can even just use a plastic folder with sleeves in it. Whatever feels good to you is perfect.

Chapter 1: Preparing for Your Journey

As a guide, below is a picture of two of my Books of Shadows. I've had the black one for over 20 years and use it to record every bit of magickal information I learn (colours, Moon phases, crystals, etc.) plus other people's rituals. I use the fancy brown one to record my own original rituals.

> A Book of Shadows is a journal that you use to record magickal information, rituals and the wisdom you've gained from the rituals you've performed.

Other supplies

I'd recommend quickly looking through the ritual in each chapter as you begin reading it and checking what you'll need. This will allow you to begin collecting the items you'll need to perform each ritual, such as candles and crystals, ahead of time.

Nothing will be very expensive and – as with the supplies above – they'll be easy to obtain online.

Creating a sacred space for your journey

You are not limited to being at home when you do this work. You can do it anywhere by simply taking this book with you. That said, when you are at home, it would be a magickal thing to do this sacred work in a sacred space.

You can read more about sacred spaces in Chapter 7. In the meantime, to prepare for your journey, I'd encourage you to simply create a special space for yourself. Make sure it's private, comfortable, uncluttered, energetically cleansed (use your smudge stick or incense) and somewhere you're happy to hang out in.

> ## My everyday sacred space
> My studio is a sacred space that doubles as my office, and I do a lot of my writing in here. I keep it tidy and cleanse it regularly. I also keep crystals, candles and other items around me that are not only useful but also pleasing to my eye. This creates an energy of comfort and relaxation that's perfect to work in.

Understanding altars

In your first ritual, which you'll find at the end of this chapter, you'll need to prepare an altar for yourself within your sacred space. In case you've never come across the concept of an altar before, here's a quick definition.

An altar is a table (or other flat surface) that you use as a focus during your rituals. On it, you'll place items that are sacred or important to you. You may like to create an altar in your sacred space, or your altar

Chapter 1: Preparing for Your Journey

can *be* the sacred space itself. You can create permanent or temporary altars anywhere and everywhere, for any purpose you need.

I have my main altar in my bedroom and one in my kitchen – and I also use Nature herself as an altar all the time. One of my friends has an altar in her lounge room for the whole family to use, and another has a mini-altar in her car!

Your altar can serve as a simple shrine, or it may be practical – containing all the tools you will need for ritual work. (You'll learn more about these tools in upcoming chapters.)

The most important thing with your altar is to go with what feels right and good for *you*. There are no set rules, so you can make it as simple or as elaborate as you wish.

Following are a few pictures of altars I've created as a guide.

Organising your time

If you don't already include the teachings in this book in your life, you'll need to make time for them. Whether you're blessed with lots of free time or have very little of it, you'll need to create space to integrate what you learn into your daily lifestyle.

I know that's easy to say... I've had phases in my life where I've juggled work, study and running a business, along with a husband and two young children. That meant I had to prioritise my time in order to still eat well, exercise, get enough sleep and practise my spirituality daily. It's not always easy to actually do, but effort will equal results.

Your journey will be your own and how you prioritise your time is up to you. However, I encourage you to look at where you can start saving time so you can devote some of it to your wholistic lifestyle and magickal practices. The ritual at the end of this chapter will help you, but here are a few additional ideas:

> Your journey will be your own and how you prioritise your time is up to you.

- **Start each day well by setting your intentions first thing.** I know that doing this helps *me* to stay focused. You might like to say them out loud or write yourself up a daily schedule and do your best to stick to it.

- **Avoid or reduce distractions.** Distractions for me are shiny, pretty things like my mates asking me out for random lunches. If I have a goal to reach, I try to keep those lunches to a minimum until I'm done! Other possible ways to reduce distractions might include:
    - watching a bit less telly (if you're a TV person)
    - reducing the amount of time you spend socialising
    - cutting back on the time you spend on social media. Also, try to only check your emails twice a day at most.

Chapter 1: Preparing for Your Journey

- 🧹 **Create daily rituals to get organised.** Some of these might include:
  - preparing meals in advance
  - getting clothes or uniforms ready the night before
  - readying any school or work supplies for the next day.
- 🧹 **Share more of your chores with other house members.** Or, if that's not possible, consider leaving non-urgent things till later. I used to get to work late almost every day because I insisted on leaving my kitchen spotless. I didn't need to, and it just created a whole lot of extra stress.
- 🧹 **Go to bed earlier so you can get up earlier.** Even 15 minutes can make a huge difference to your day. Or, on the other hand, if you're a night owl, stay up a bit later and make sure you use the time well.

Even devoting ten minutes a day to your wholistic lifestyle can make a huge difference in the long term.

Awareness: starting your journey with clarity

> Becoming aware of where you're out of balance, then taking action to rebalance moves you ever closer to achieving a wholistic lifestyle.

At its core, this book is all about wholistic living, which I define as living with your mind, body and soul in harmony and alignment. Becoming aware of where you're out of balance, then taking action to rebalance moves you ever closer to achieving a wholistic lifestyle. This greatly impacts not only your daily life but also your wellbeing and your magick.

On a personal level, it also helps you to reconnect with your truth, your wild self, your intuition and your innermost desires. This then allows you to live an unashamedly authentic life, which is the ultimate goal for most of us.

Through my own experiences, I've developed what I believe to be the five keys to living a wholistic lifestyle. Following, I share why each one is important and then take you through a short quiz to help you see which areas you may need to give more energy to.

This will help you to begin your journey with clarity so you'll know where to start.

The five keys to living a wholistic lifestyle

Good nutrition

Food is medicine for both your body and your soul. It nourishes you, giving you fuel to survive and energy to thrive. That's why keeping your food as clean as possible is essential for overall health and wellbeing.

Packaged, processed and takeaway foods are often full of chemicals, sugar, additives and preservatives that can have a negative effect on your mind, body and soul. Clean food equals clean energy, and clean energy is good for your magick, as it keeps your vibration buzzing high.

Adequate sleep

You regenerate when you sleep, so getting as many hours as you can is essential for a healthy mind and body. Nourishing sleep can also help you progress on your personal and spiritual paths. When you're asleep, your intuition is free to tune in and expand, so you can travel to other realms and find the answers to pressing issues through dream journeying.

Everyone's sleep requirements will be different, so if you don't already pay attention, start noticing how much sleep you need to function well. I love to get my eight hours, but sometimes I'm totally buzzing from six.

Chapter 1: Preparing for Your Journey

Lots of water

I feel like water is common sense, but some people really struggle with this. Water is life, and you need it to cleanse you, nurture and replenish your organs and feed your cells.

If you struggle with drinking enough water, maybe try drinking more herbal teas. You can also 'eat your water' with water-rich foods such as cucumber, watermelon, lettuce, tomato, celery and spinach.

Daily movement

I personally am an exercise nut, so it's easy for me to find ways to move my body. If you don't love activity, the key is to find something you enjoy. You have to make it fun so that you want to keep doing it!

My favourite fun forms of exercise include:

- roller-skating
- kickboxing with friends or family
- swimming
- weight training
- playing at the park
- yoga
- walking in Nature with friends or family
- outdoor gyms
- dancing.

Exercise keeps you and your organs fit and functioning well. It also releases endorphins (happy brain chemicals), helps with weight control and keeps your muscles nice and strong.

For excellent health benefits, improved wellbeing and a higher vibration, aim for a minimum of thirty minutes three times a week.

Nurturing the soul

It's imperative to give as much energy to nourishing your soul as you do to nourishing your mind and body. Things that do this might include:

- rest
- meditation
- journalling
- spending time with people who uplift you
- reading
- listening to music
- healing
- daily ritual
- uplifting movies
- getting out in Nature.

Try to do at least one thing every day that brings you joy, contentment and happiness.

> It's imperative to give as much energy to nourishing your soul as you do to nourishing your mind and body.

Quiz time!

Now let's take a little quiz to highlight any areas you may need to give more energy to. This is a handy tool to help you pinpoint areas of your life and/or health where you might need to make improvements to support your overall wellbeing.

Give yourself a rating to answer each question below as honestly as possible. Then follow the instructions at the end to calculate your score. Once you have your result, create an action plan to make any changes you need in your daily life. For example, start to schedule in exercise if you don't do any or don't do enough.

Chapter 1: Preparing for Your Journey

1. How would you rate your eating habits? (please circle)

1–4 Pretty terrible. I eat lots of processed food, takeaway foods and sugar, with very little fruit and veggies. I also eat irregular meals, and my portions could be better.

Comments: _____

_____

_____

5–7 Pretty good. I eat at least three mostly home-cooked meals a day, although I use packets or jarred foods sometimes. Takeaway is a fairly regular treat (maybe once a week) and I also enjoy a sugary treat, eg. chocolate or biscuits, most days. I try to include veggies and fruit in my diet most days, and my portions are OK.

Comments: _____

_____

_____

8–10 Totally excellent! I rarely (or never) eat processed foods, takeaway food or sugar, and I include loads of veggies and fruit in my daily diet. I eat at least four or five times a day and my portions suit my needs.

Comments: _____

_____

_____

_____

2. How much water do you drink each day?

None, unless it's in something else (eg. tea or cordial) ☐

1–3 glasses ☐   4–7 glasses ☐   8+ glasses ☐

3. How often do you move your body?

Never ☐   1–3 times a week ☐   4–6 times a week ☐

7+ times a week ☐

4. What sort of exercise do you like to do?

None, I hate exercise ☐   Mild – walking, yoga, light weights ☐

Moderate – swimming, bike-riding, brisk walking or hiking, weights, dancing ☐

Intense – boxing/martial arts, running, extreme sport (eg. rock climbing), vigorous dancing ☐

5. How much sleep do you get most nights?

3-4 hours ☐   5–7 hours ☐   8+ hours ☐

6. How much time do you spend work working?

I don't work ☐   5–15 hours ☐   16–30 hours ☐

31–50 hours ☐   51+ Hours ☐

7. Do you make time to rest each day?   Yes ☐   No ☐

8. Do you regularly take time out to just be still and quiet?

Yes ☐   No ☐

Chapter 1: Preparing for Your Journey

9. Do you regularly take time for activities that make you laugh and bring you joy?

Yes ☐   No ☐

10. Do you regularly take time out to commune with Nature?

Yes ☐   No ☐

11. Are your relationships with friends and family loving, supportive and nourishing for your soul? Do they lift you up and light you up?

Yes ☐   No ☐

12. Do you take time every day to nurture your spiritual practices?

Yes ☐   No ☐

Now go back through your answers and give yourself a point for each area where you honestly feel that you're doing well. Add up the points to give yourself a score out of 12.

If you scored over seven, you're well on your way to living a wholistic lifestyle, but there's always room for improvement. And whether you scored well or not, take note of any areas where you're doing less well, so you can give more energy to these throughout this journey.

Make some notes below:

_____

_____

_____

_____

This chapter should give you an understanding of the basics of a wholistic, healthy lifestyle, and why it's important. Now you're armed with the knowledge you need to make any necessary changes.

From Chapter 2 onward, we'll switch focus from the physical to the spiritual realm. However, it's important to keep working on these five areas on your own as you continue your journey through the book.

The ritual below will help you to dedicate the time and energy you need to make any changes within your daily life. This will then allow you to more fully immerse yourself in your journey.

Your ritual work: making space for your Self

This ritual will help you to find the time and motivation to integrate wholistic practices into your daily life. It doesn't matter whether you're a beginner or an adept at magick – I've kept the spell simple for you with items that are easy to obtain.

Intentions

- Clear some clutter from your schedule.
- Organise your time.
- Prepare your mindset for this work.
- Make space in your daily routine for this work.

Timing

Perform on a Saturday, preferably during a Waxing Moon (see Chapter 3 on cycles to understand this timing).

You will need

- A handful of salt.
- Your journal, Book of Shadows or a piece of paper.
- A pen.

Chapter 1: Preparing for Your Journey

- Candles in red, green and white.
- A sage stick or palo santo stick.

Ritual steps

1. Prepare and cleanse the space where you'll perform the spell. Make sure it's private and that you won't be disturbed (you can totally do this outside too!)
2. Have a bath or shower. As you do, mix the salt with a little water to make a paste and use it as a scrub to thoroughly cleanse yourself of toxins and negativity. Imagine them all washing away with the water down the drain.
3. Get out and pat yourself dry. Stay natural for this ritual: don't wear creams, deodorants or perfumes.
4. Sit before your altar or in the sacred space you've created for yourself.
5. First, light the white candle. This is the sacred altar candle and your focus candle. Then light the green candle for the Goddess and the red candle for the God.
6. Imagine your whole space being surrounded by a big circle of white light. This is to keep you safe and protected while you do your spellwork. Alternatively, if you're experienced with ritual, you may like to do your own type of circle casting.
7. Take a few moments to breathe and focus on the intentions of this spell.
8. Take your journal/paper and write down what a typical day's schedule looks like for you. Be really honest with yourself: include things like scoping social media and watching TV. Get really detailed. Also, note your daily habits – what time do you generally go to bed and get up?
9. Carefully look over your list. Is there anything you can cut out or reduce? Can you cut down on phone time or check your emails less often? Can you watch a little less TV or get up half an hour earlier?

10. On a separate page or piece of paper, write down a loose new schedule. Include things like a morning meditation or ritual, exercise, meal prep, rest time, sleep, etc.

11. Read over your list three times, getting it really clear in your mind and setting your intention. After you've read it, say something like the following:

> *"I hereby set my new intentions into motion*
> *I declare these without fuss or commotion*
> *I integrate my new lifestyle with grace and ease*
> *In order to help me live the wholistic life I please*
> *These words carry with them the*
> *power of three times three*
> *My intentions are set, so mote it be."*

12. Sleep with your new schedule under your pillow. Every morning for the next seven days at least (or until you feel you've fully integrated it), read your new schedule out loud to the Universe. Then actually DO the new practices you've scheduled in.

Start slow if you need to so you don't experience overwhelm, but do start.

Your spell is complete.

Integrating these teachings into your wholistic lifestyle

> The most important thing is to make the time for this journey.

🧹 **The most important thing is to make the time for this journey.** So begin with becoming aware of how you spend your time each day. Make notes if you think it will help you to gain clarity.

Chapter 1: Preparing for Your Journey

- **Immediately begin to make adjustments to any areas that the quiz has helped you realise you need to change** – nutrition, rest, etc. Again, go slow if it feels overwhelming.
- **Begin collecting the items you'll need for your journey.** Keep a lookout for items and tools you might be able to use for your altar, sacred space or within your daily life. I've often found the most amazing things when I wasn't actually looking for them, just by staying aware and open at places like garage sales or op shops.
- **If you don't journal already, get into the habit.** Even a sentence or two each day is enough to begin with until it feels natural.

Book of Shadows

For this chapter, please record your first ritual.

If your Book of Shadows is new, you might also like to spend some time laying it out in a way that pleases you. For example, you might want to make a section for magickal info and another for rituals.

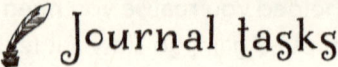

> ## ✒ Journal tasks
>
> Throughout this book, I'll ask you to answer questions, record your thoughts and share your daydreams — hence the need for a journal.
>
> I encourage you to complete these journalling exercises, as they're a practical tool designed to help you evolve and expand during your journey.
>
> For this chapter, please record your observations from the quiz.

Summary - Chapter 1

- 🧙 Before embarking on any journey, it's essential to prepare for it.
- 🧙 To prepare for your wholistic witchcraft journey, you'll need a few inexpensive tools.
- 🧙 To begin your journey with clarity, you'll need to understand the foundations of wholistic health, which encompass nutrition, sleep, hydration, exercise and activities that nurture your soul.
- 🧙 You'll also need to understand how you're doing with each of these foundations and be prepared to rebalance in areas that need more energy.

CHAPTER 2
Energy Work

Understanding energy

One of the most important things to know when you begin your magickal journey is that everything – and I mean *everything* – is energy. And it's all connected.

To get the most out of this book and your magickal journey, it's important to understand your own energy and how to make that energy work best for you. It's also important to understand how focusing your intention creates the right kind of energy. In short: if you want to make a lifestyle or personal change – or just get a spell to work – you need to put the right energy and intention behind it.

Throughout this book, you'll learn all about different energetic influences and how to use them. However, this chapter focuses on your *own* energy. We'll talk about how to feel it and how to keep it flowing beautifully to achieve the best outcome in everything you do.

We'll also talk about your body's energy centres (chakras) and discuss how to protect your energy. This is particularly useful and important if you're an empath or when you're doing any spellwork.

How to keep your personal energy vibrating high

> The first step to understanding your own energy is getting to know how it *feels*.

The first step to understanding your own energy is getting to know how it *feels*. Do you remember rubbing your hands together really fast and then pulling them apart as a kid? Remember how it felt as though your hands were magnets? (And if you haven't done this, give it a go right now!)

Well, that was energy. That tingling, pulling sensation is what your personal energy feels like.

It's important to realise that your energy won't be high all the time. Instead, it will naturally flow – and you can get to know it by noticing when it's high and when it's low. For example, notice:

- 🧙 which foods make you feel energised and which make you feel heavy and sluggish
- 🧙 whether you experience tingling in your hands or other parts of your body (like goosebumps or feeling as if your hair is standing on end)
- 🧙 how you feel when you're moving.

Once you understand your personal energy, you can begin to work with its flows. For example, it's best to move your body, work on a creative project or do your rituals when your energy is high. The best time to rest, reflect, journal or meditate is probably when your energy is lower.

When you're working through the rituals in this book, you'll mostly do them when your energy is high. If you notice that it's feeling lower,

however, the best way to improve and then maintain it is by practising the five keys we discussed in Chapter 1:

- good nutrition
- adequate sleep
- lots of water
- daily movement
- activities to nurture your soul.

Focusing on these five keys will put you well on your way to raising your energy.

Other magickal ways to raise your energy

- Cleanse your home with a smudge stick and/or burn essential oils.
- Eat lots of leafy greens.
- Listen to uplifting music. It doesn't matter what genre you're into (I love heavy metal) – if it makes you happy and energises you, pump it out! You could also:
  - dance and/or sing
  - play a singing bowl, some drums or any other instrument.
- Meditate and connect with your breath.
- Heal and clear feelings of anger, resentment and guilt, and practise forgiveness.
- Spend time in Nature.
- Bask in the healing rays of the Sun.
- Do some invigorating exercise.
- Hang out with people who uplift and inspire you.
- Spread love and practise kindness.
- Read or watch something inspiring.
- Do things that make you smile and laugh.

Your chakras

I started working with chakras about two years ago, and it's had a profoundly positive effect for me, both with my energy work and magick.

The word 'chakra' means 'wheel' or 'circle' in Sanskrit. There are seven *main* chakras, or energy centres, in your body. Each one is a swirling vortex that draws spiritual energy into your energy field (also known as your aura).

It's important to keep your chakras harmonised and balanced, as they're essential for wellbeing and wholeness. If one isn't functioning correctly, it can throw your whole energy and health off-balance.

For example, each chakra is also located close to one of your body's endocrine centres and is associated with its hormonal function. Your body can process the spiritual energy that the chakra emits, turning it into usable healing energy for physical, emotional or spiritual wellness.

The seven chakras

Each chakra maps to a specific place on your physical body and is associated with its own colour.

Here's a quick rundown of each main chakra and the energy it governs.

1. **Base chakra – red.** Located at the base of your spine, this is your centre of survival, balance, safety, strength and grounding.
2. **Sacral chakra – orange.** Located approximately 4cm below your belly button, it's your centre of passion, creativity, sexuality, fire and joy.

3. **Solar plexus chakra – yellow.** Sitting between your belly button and sternum, it's your centre of intuition, trust, decisions and personal power.
4. **Heart chakra – green or baby pink.** Located at your heart centre, this is your source of love – both for yourself and for others.
5. **Throat chakra – indigo blue.** Located at the base of your throat in the dip above your collar bone, it's the seat of truth, communication, self-expression and willpower.
6. **Third eye chakra – purple.** Located right between your eyes just above your brow area, this is your centre of knowing, clairvoyance (clear seeing) and higher powers.
7. **Crown chakra – white.** Sitting just above the centre of your head, this chakra is your connection to the Divine, source and light.

Except for the heart chakra, each of the seven main chakras also has a corresponding chakra. This means that when you work with one chakra, it can open and affect another one. Closely linked chakras include:

- the base and crown chakras
- the third eye and sacral chakras
- the solar plexus and throat chakras.

Other chakra associations

- **Elements:** working with chakras will heighten your awareness of the elements around you, as each chakra corresponds to a particular element.
- **Sense:** each chakra is associated with a physical sense, and working with them may help to heighten your senses.
- **Symbols:** each chakra has its own symbol, and meditating on the symbol can bring new energy into that chakra.
- **Lotus:** each chakra is represented by a pattern of lotus petals, and meditating on these lotuses can help to harmonise your chakras.

The following table lists the specific element, sense, symbol and lotus that's associated with each chakra.

	Chakra 1	Chakra 2	Chakra 3	Chakra 4	Chakra 5	Chakra 6	Chakra 7
Known as (Sanskrit name)	Base (Muladhara)	Sacral (Swadhisthana)	Solar plexus (Manipura)	Heart (Anahata)	Throat (Vishuddha)	Third eye (Ajna)	Crown (Sahasrara)
Location	Base of the spine	4cm below the naval	Centre of the stomach below the rib cage	Centre of the chest: the heart	Throat area: front and back of the neck and shoulders	Centre of the brow and back of the head	Just above the top of the head
Element	Earth	Water	Fire	Air	Akasha – sky and Aether	Light	Thought
Sense	Smell and taste	Taste	Sight	Touch	Hearing	The sixth sense	None
Symbol	Square	Crescent moon	Circle with inverted equilateral triangle	Six-pointed star within a circle	Circle within a downward pointed triangle within a larger circle	Twin petals representing the Sun and Moon (and the manifest and unmanifest mind)	1,000-petalled lotus or rose
Lotus petals	4 petals	6 petals	10 petals	12 petals	16 petals	96 petals	1,000 petals

Chapter 2: Energy Work

Working with your chakras

To learn more about your chakras and how to work with them to increase your energy, I'd suggest the following approaches:

- **Reading:** starting with the base chakra, read whatever you can about each chakra to understand them more. You may want to start by simply Googling each chakra or refer to Appendix I for books I recommend.

- **Meditating:** if you're just starting out working with your chakras, I'd recommend working with one at a time. This allows you to really connect with each chakra and feel into how it works.

    If you have some knowledge or have worked with chakras before, you can focus on balancing one chakra at a time. For example, you could specifically work with your sacral chakra if you're in need of more creative energy. Or you could do a full body chakra balance meditation.

    If you need guidance, you might like to try my chakra meditation (see Appendix I) or search chakra meditations on YouTube.

- **Paying attention:** when you're doing breath or meditation work with your chakras, notice any feelings – physical or emotional – or words, visuals or messages you receive. These will often be a sign that you're really tuning in to that chakra and energising it.

- **Balancing chakras:** if one particular chakra seems out of harmony, surround yourself with its corresponding colour. You could wear that colour, buy flowers or soft furnishings in it, or burn candles or eat foods of that colour. For example, if you're feeling anxious and unsafe, chances are that your base chakra is out of balance, so you'd surround yourself with red.

- **Using essential oils:** massage a chakra-related oil blend directly onto your skin in the area over a chakra, or burn essential oils that stimulate that chakra in your home. My favourite oils are by Spiritual Healing House – find their details in Appendix I.

Note: please take care when you use any essential oil. Make sure you aren't allergic to it, and always blend pure oils with a suitable base oil first. Also, follow the instructions on the label, and consult a natural healthcare professional if you're unsure.

- **Using crystals:** empower a chakra-related crystal with your energy and intention and then carry it with you. To empower my crystals, I like to speak into them or simply hold them while thinking about what I want them to do. You can carry a specific crystal for just one chakra or many at the same time. Whatever you feel you need is right.

The importance of protecting your energy

As magickal beings, we can sometimes be susceptible to external energies. And when I say 'external energies', I'm not talking about Nature's energy or the Moon's energy here. Instead, I'm talking about energy from other humans, spirits and entities (spirits that haven't passed over).

When you're vibrating high, spirits and entities can be attracted to your light like moths to a flame. Or, adversely, they may cling to you like parasites when your energy is low or depleted because your defences are down, making you an 'easy target'.

Plus, if you're an empath like me, you can pick up on other people's energies – both good and bad – very easily. And if you don't know how to protect yourself, you can take these energies *into* yourself or your aura. This can then make it very difficult to keep your own energy in flow and will also affect any magickal work you do.

Chapter 2: Energy Work

The good news is that it's relatively simple to protect your own energy. One of the simplest methods, which I've used for years, is creating a protective bubble of white light.

> The good news is that it's relatively simple to protect your own energy.

The 'bubble of white light' technique

Surrounding yourself with white light protects you from any negative energies from humans or entities that are hanging around. You can also bring the light into yourself or open it within you.

I most often use this technique for protection during my rituals if I need to go to busy public places or when I'm travelling. And because I've been doing it for a long time, I can now conjure a bubble anytime and anywhere. As I was learning, however, I needed to use one of the visualisations below – and I often still use them.

Whichever option you choose, start by sitting or lying somewhere private and comfortable with your eyes closed. Then use one or more of these techniques:

- **Take several deep breaths and imagine a ring of white light above you.** See this ring showering beautiful light down over you. Then take the light within yourself until it fills every cell in your body to the brim and you *become* light. Imagine your skin glowing with it.
- **Ask your angels or guides to surround and protect you with a ball of the light.** When you can see and feel yourself within this large ball, see your angels filling it up with pure white light in a burst of power. Again, take this light within yourself and let it fill you until you become it.
- **Create a sphere of white light to surround and protect you and your sacred space when you're ready to perform a ritual.** Call on your angels/guides/the Universe/the God or Goddess to bring this light to you and then extend it into a large sphere that connects into the Earth beneath you and the space above you.

- 🧙 **Take a few deep breaths and focus on your centre.** As you do so, visualise a white flower within you. Watch it opening, petal by petal, as pure white light pours out of it, filling you until you're glowing with it.

- 🧙 **Sit or stand with your spine straight, and imagine being pulled upright by a string from the top of your head.** Now call cosmic energy to you through the crown of your head. Feel yourself filled with pure white light from head to toe in every cell of your body – again, until you become the light.

Try practising each of these methods or create a technique yourself.

Other ways to protect your energy

- 🧙 Use protective crystals like black tourmaline, onyx, obsidian or tiger's eye. Again, empower the crystal and carry it with you (crystal jewellery is good for this).
- 🧙 Smudge yourself and your home.
- 🧙 Hang a broomstick upside down over your front door to deflect negative energies.
- 🧙 Call on your guides to protect you.

Your ritual work: casting a circle

> A circle is a safe, sacred space that you create to perform your magick within — a space in which you can contain and raise energy.

A circle is a safe, sacred space that you create to perform your magick within – a space in which you can contain and raise energy. Creating a circle also helps to prevent negative entities from latching onto you while you're working closely with the otherworld and otherworldly energies.

That's why you'll cast a circle at the start of every ritual in this book. How big you make your circle is really up to you, although they're traditionally about nine feet in

Chapter 2: Energy Work

diameter. You can also cast yours indoors or out, and you can mark it out in various ways. For example:

- **For an outdoor ritual,** you can mark your circle out with a sword or athame (magick knife), or use salt.
- **For an indoor ritual,** you can use chalk, salt or a white cord.
- **If you have a permanent space,** you could be really bold and mark out your circle permanently with paint.

Of course, you don't *have* to do any of these things. If you prefer, you can simply visualise a circle of white light, which – as I mentioned above – is what I most often do.

Intention

To create a circle of safe, protected, sacred space.

Timing

Perform this ritual at any time.

You will need

- Salt in a bowl to represent Earth.
- Water in a bowl to represent Water.
- God (red) and Goddess (green) candles.
- Four white candles to mark the directions (North, East, South and West).
- A smudge stick or palo santo stick to represent Air.
- A lighter or matches.
- Athame or wand if you have one.

Ritual steps

1. Set up a small altar with your tools for the ritual and your Goddess and God representations.
2. Cleanse yourself and your space with the smudge stick or palo santo stick, then light your candles and begin.

3. Mark the directions by placing white candles just outside the perimeter of the circle, then light them.

4. Using your finger (or your athame/wand if you have one), hold your arm straight out in front of you and point your finger/knife.

   Begin to walk a line widdershins (anti-clockwise) around the circle if you're in the Southern Hemisphere, or deosil (clockwise) if you're in the Northern Hemisphere. As you walk, visualise white light streaming out of your finger/knife. See a ring of white light forming and expanding, both above and below the line.

   As it forms, say three times:

   > *"I conjure you, circle, to provide me with a*
   > *safe and sacred space to work within.*
   > *So mote it be."*

   By the time you're back to where you started, see the white light extending up all the way to the ceiling and down below the ground/floor in a large sphere all around you.

5. Walk the circle four times, once with each of your elemental representations. As you walk each circle:
   ★ first sprinkle some of the water from your bowl
   ★ then sprinkle a little of the salt
   ★ next swirl the smoke from the smudge stick around
   ★ finally (carefully) carry one of the candles.

6. Call in the Goddess and God by saying:

   > *"Goddess and God of all that is.*
   > *I ask you to witness and bless this magickal working*
   > *that is set outside of time within this sacred space.*
   > *Blessed be."*

   If you're asking a particular goddess and/or god to attend your ritual, you can substitute their name/s for the 'Goddess and God' above.

Chapter 2: Energy Work

Your circle is now ready for your ritual.

7. When you've completed your spell, thank the directions and the Goddess and God.
8. Now walk deosil around the circle if you're in the Southern Hemisphere, or widdershins if you're in the Northern Hemisphere. Walk pointing your hand/knife at the centre to 'cut' the circle. Visualise the white light dissipating and say:

"The circle is open but never broken."

Now that you understand your energy, how it works and how to protect it, you're ready to begin the rest of your work.

Integrating these teachings into your wholistic lifestyle

- Start noticing how your energy ebbs and flows throughout the day.
- Get into the practice of surrounding yourself with a bubble of white light whenever you leave your house.
- Pay conscious attention to what you eat and drink, and how it makes you feel.
- Start practising some of the energy-raising exercises listed earlier in this chapter.
- Spend more time out in Nature tuning in to her energies, and notice if they affect you.

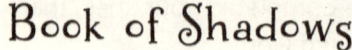

Book of Shadows

☽ Record ways you can raise your energy (include your own ideas/methods).

☽ Record information on chakras.

☽ Record ways to protect your energy.

☽ Record your experience of casting a circle and what you observe afterwards.

Journal tasks

From this moment forward, start being aware of your energy. In particular, notice (and make notes on) how it ebbs and flows, including:

🜋 What gives you more energy?

🜋 What zaps it?

🜋 When are your high points throughout the day? When are your low points?

🜋 How can you improve your energy during low points?

🜋 What can you do right now to improve your energy?

Also journal any observations from your ritual work.

Chapter 2: Energy Work

Summary – Chapter 2

- 🧹 Everything is energy, and everything is connected.
- 🧹 The five keys of a wholistic lifestyle from Chapter 1 create a foundation for keeping your energy high.
- 🧹 Beyond this, working with your chakras will help to raise and maintain your energy.
- 🧹 One of the simplest techniques to protect your energy involves creating a bubble of white light.

CHAPTER 3

Cycles

There are cycles all around you

Everything is cyclic: the Moon orbiting the Earth, the seasons, the sabbats, the tides, animal behaviours, the growth and harvesting of crops, and the rhythms of your body. And every cycle has its own energy ebbs and flows.

> Every cycle has its own energy ebbs and flows.

Understanding and working with these cycles, especially the cycles of Nature and your body, enables you to use their energy flows for your wellbeing and magick.

In this chapter, you'll learn about many of these cycles. You'll start with the cycles of the year (seasons), then move to monthly cycles (the Moon), weekly cycles (days) and daily cycles (times).

You'll also discover how to tune in to these cycles, both consciously and unconsciously. And, finally, we'll discuss how to observe your own cycles and align them with those of Nature to enhance your wholistic lifestyle.

Yearly cycles – living by the seasons

As Mother Nature moves through each season, she brings with her continuous transformation. This creates changes in temperature, weather patterns, plant life, foods, daylight/darkness and both animal and human behaviour. The constantly shifting energy influences all of these changes, and learning to live in harmony with the shifts can benefit you both personally and within your magickal practice.

Have you ever noticed that as the seasons change, so too do your own habits? For example, in summer, most people get up earlier, eat lighter foods and get outside more. Then, in winter, they tend to like to snuggle up inside with a bowl of steaming hot comfort food.

Just like animals, we instinctively know what we need to survive the hot or cool months. Sadly, though, many humans in modern societies just push through each day as though it were the same as any other. They don't understand what it truly means to live in harmony with the energies and gifts that each season brings.

One of my favourite quotes by Henry David Thoreau sums it up beautifully:

> *"Live each season as it passes; breathe the air, drink the drink, taste the fruit, and resign yourself to the influences of each."*

Let's take a closer look at how to tune in to seasonal energies, understand them and integrate them into your wholistic lifestyle.

Spring

This part of the yearly cycle lasts from the Spring Equinox to the Summer Solstice.

Associations

- **Direction:** East.
- **Colour:** Yellow.
- **Element:** Air, which brings the energy of change and growth.

Chapter 3: Cycles

Energy

Abundance, change, cleansing, fertility, fresh starts, growth, hope and new beginnings.

Best ways to harness spring energies

- Give your home a spring clean and then a spring blessing. Consecrate it with Earth, Fire, Air and Water.
- Give your body a spring clean with a good detox. Cleanse away any residual 'heaviness' from winter by nourishing your body with fresh seasonal food that's sacred to spring.
- Honour your body. As the season changes, your body will begin to develop different needs. You may find yourself wanting:
  - more hydration (ie. water) for your body and less for your skin (ie. a lighter moisturiser)
  - body scrubs to remove any buildup of dead skin cells from winter.
- Start new things/new projects. These can include new relationships of any kind or beginning to manifest your desires.
- Get out in Nature more. Raise your seasonal awareness by drinking in all the new plant and animal life. This is also a good time to plant your spring seeds – make it ritualistic by asking for blessings and paying homage to Mother Earth.
- Bless babies and children. This is a good time for naming ceremonies too.
- Work on matters where you need a positive outcome. These might include a legal situation or finding a new job.
- Make sure you're thinking abundantly. After all, this is a time of abundance in Nature.

Things to place on your altar or in your sacred space

First of all, give your altar and sacred space a good spring clean!

Then decorate it with any (or all) of the following:

- eggs
- feathers
- leaves with buds on them
- pots of seedlings
- representations of rabbits, butterflies or birds
- spring flowers, vegetables or herbs
- a representation of the Sun
- a yellow altar cloth
- yellow or white candles, or yellow crystals or flowers.

Also, if there are any windows near your altar, open them up and let the fresh spring air circulate!

Summer

This part of the yearly cycle lasts from the Summer Solstice to the Autumn Equinox.

Associations

- **Direction:** South.
- **Colours:** Red, green, yellow and orange.
- **Element:** Fire.

Energy

Achievement, celebration, connection, creativity, fire, fun, joy and pleasure, motivation, passion and success.

Best ways to harness summer energies

- **Nourish your body and skin.** Eat light, fresh, seasonal summer food, drink lots of water, and use body scrubs and light moisturisers.

Chapter 3: Cycles

- 🌿 **Indulge in lots of outdoor activities for fitness.** Focus especially on the ones that bring you joy, fun and pleasure.
- 🌿 **Create, create, create.** Nurture and work on the projects you began in spring. Also use this energy to create success and happiness in your career.
- 🌿 **Get outside more.** Strengthen your connection to Nature and be aware of the changes that are happening around you. For example, connect with the power of the Sun, and utilise sun energies – which are at *their peak* – for your magickal work and healing.
- 🌿 **Connect more with your partner, family and friends.** This is a great time for outdoor get-togethers with people you care about. It's also the perfect energy to fire up your passion with your partner; and, if you're trying to conceive, it's the best time to improve fertility.
- 🌿 **Travel.** This is a great time to head to cooler climates if you're like me and don't love the heat!
- 🌿 **Get to know yourself on a deeper level.** Learn what your strengths are, claim your identity and settle into your truth. Work with your solar plexus chakra (see Chapter 2) to help you with this, as it's the seat of your personal power.
- 🌿 **Harvest your bountiful crops.** This applies both literally (in the garden) and metaphorically to other projects in your life.

Things to place on your altar or in your sacred space

- 🌿 brightly coloured flowers
- 🌿 fresh herbs and harvested fruits or vegetables
- 🌿 gold coins or golden fern pollen, which legend claims will reveal buried treasure wherever it falls
- 🌿 orange or red candles
- 🌿 an orange, green or red altar cloth
- 🌿 red, orange or yellow ribbons
- 🌿 representations of the Sun, or a sun goddess or god

- summer crystals like citrine, garnet, carnelian or sunstone
- tools associated with fire, such as candles or a cauldron.

Autumn

This part of the yearly cycle lasts from the Autumn Equinox to the Winter Solstice.

Associations

- **Direction**: West.
- **Colour**: Blue.
- **Element**: Water.

Energy

Celebrating successes, gratitude, harmony, nurturing relationships, reconciliation, reflection, stability and winding down.

Best ways to harness autumn energies

- **Nourish your body and skin.** Eat fresh, seasonal autumn foods, keep drinking lots of water and switch to a normal moisturiser. Avoid putting anything too heavy on your skin at night.
- **Hold a large feast for family and friends.** Use fresh produce from the last summer harvest, and then preserve/store what you can for winter.
- **Cast protection and harmony spells for your home.** You may start spending more time indoors soon, so this is a good time for reconciliation and improving relationships.
- **Practice gratitude daily for all the blessings summer gave you.** Also recognise your own successes and the work you've put in over the year.
- **Begin winding down and finishing up.** In particular, look at finishing up the projects you've been working on over spring and summer. It's also a good time to secure your finances and work on bringing your long-term goals to fruition.

Chapter 3: Cycles

- **Begin preparing for winter.** Air out your blankies and warm clothes, collect wood if you have a fireplace, store food and do a final clean up/declutter of your garden.

Things to place on your altar or in your sacred space

- autumnal fruits that have been harvested
- autumnal leaves in all the colours
- a blue altar cloth or blue candles
- coins in copper or bronze
- statues of geese or a stag
- a water feature
- wheat or barley
- woven grasses (my husband wove me a pentagram out of grass, which is pretty cool).

Winter

This part of the yearly cycle lasts from the Winter Solstice to the Spring Equinox.

Associations

- **Direction:** North.
- **Colour:** Green.
- **Element:** Earth.

Energy

Clarity, comfort, creation, hibernation, home harmony, insight, learning, new beginnings, planning, releasing and transformation.

Best ways to harness winter energies

- **Nourish your body.** Eat warming winter harvest foods like root veggies, nuts and seeds, meats, soups, casseroles, homemade breads, etc.

- 🧹 **Nourish your skin.** Drink lots of water, try dry skin brushing and moisturise morning and night. Pay particular attention to your elbows, knees, hands and feet.
- 🧹 **Cast spells for your hearth and home.** In particular, look at harmony or protection spells. This is also an excellent time to really connect with your family.
- 🧹 **Do your inner work.** In particular, it's a good time for shadow work (see Chapter 12) and increasing your psychic powers.
- 🧹 **Let go of what's unneeded.** Use winter energy to end situations that no longer serve you, and remove unwanted influences from your life.
- 🧹 **Hibernate, reflect and gather your strength.** Go within to connect with your deep inner wisdom and find clarity. Reflect on the seeds you planted back in spring and what you harvested from them.

  What were your triumphs? What else do you need to let go of? What do you need to give more energy to? This is a potent time to do lots of journalling.
- 🧹 **Plan.** While winter is a time of rest, it's also a good time to start planning your new beginnings for spring. Additionally, you may want to make long-term plans for money.

Things to place on your altar or in your sacred space

- 🧹 pine cones
- 🧹 red and green (or gold and silver) candles to represent the Goddess and God
- 🧹 representations of the Sun
- 🧹 seasonal fruits and veggies
- 🧹 winter greenery.

You might also like to have a small pine log burning in a fireplace or in your cauldron when you perform any rituals.

Chapter 3: Cycles

Monthly cycles – tuning in to the Moon

The Moon's cycles play an important role in our daily lives and magick, as her energies change with each phase. If the Moon can control the ocean, for example, imagine how much energetic power she has to affect everything else on Earth!

Imagine too how much effect these energies can have on us and our own cycles.

The Waxing (or increasing) Moon

This cycle phase lasts from when the crescent of the Moon first appears in the sky to the day of the Full Moon.

Energy

The Waxing Moon brings with her increasing energy, so this is a good time to work on projects and perform rituals for anything you wish to increase or attract.

It's also a great time to increase the intensity of your exercise routine and get stuff done around the house or garden. Finally, it's the time to action any plans you made during the Dark and New Moon phases.

Best ways to harness these energies

As the Moon gets closer to full, her energies intensify, so it's a great time to perform rituals for:

- new beginnings, especially new relationships – new friends and new loves
- improving your health and increasing fertility
- working on a long-term goal and making plans
- manifesting your desires and attracting things to you
- prosperity, abundance and gaining employment – especially gaining a specific job you want

- stepping into or standing in your power
- increasing your psychic powers
- good luck.

The Full Moon

This cycle phase lasts from moonrise to moonset on the night of the Full Moon.

Energy

The Full Moon is when energies are at their peak, so this is a good time to complete projects and perform rituals that need a burst of power. It's also a great time to get your house in order to prepare for the decreasing energy and motivation of the Waning Moon. Finally, it's a good time to prepare to release anything that no longer serves you.

Best ways to harness these energies

On this day, the Moon is at her most powerful, so perform rituals for:

- physical protection
- boosting your personal power and confidence on the spot
- shedding light on a troubling situation or feeling
- making a commitment to someone
- increasing sexual powers, and ensuring your partner's fidelity, especially if things are a little rough
- getting something you need immediately, eg. manifesting some urgently needed cash
- completing projects or completing a deal, eg. buying a new car
- fulfilling your goals and ambitions, eg. gaining a promotion
- travel, changing career or moving house
- consecrating your magickal tools
- bringing justice to a situation
- healing
- releasing things.

Chapter 3: Cycles

>  Handy tip
>
> On this day, the Moon is fully opposite to the Sun, so be aware that the energies can be a bit tumultuous and unstable.

The Waning Moon

This cycle phase lasts from the day after the Full Moon to the day the Moon becomes dark.

Energy

The energy of the Waning Moon is decreasing, so this is a good time to turn your focus to self-care and nurturing. It's also a great time to connect with family and friends, clear your garden of any clutter, and cast spells for banishing or releasing.

Best ways to harness these energies

The Waning Moon is excellent for rituals such as:

- removing anger, tension and disharmony from your home or workplace
- removing negative people or influences from your life
- banishing jealousy and spite from others
- banishing negative thoughts and beliefs, debt, grudges, anger, guilt and anxiety
- destroying blocks to your success and happiness
- ending relationships with love
- releasing pain, illness or excess unhealthy weight
- letting go of addictions and destructive behaviours
- accepting things you can't change in order to move forward.

The Dark and New Moons

This cycle phase lasts for the 2.5 days in which the Moon fully disappears. When she appears again, the New Moon begins and the cycle continues.

Energy

Dark Moon energy is slow and a little stagnant.

Best ways to harness these energies

The Dark Moon is the time to:

- go within
- journal and plan for the month ahead
- nurture yourself and rest
- cast spells to work with your shadow aspects or honour your crone energy.

The Moon and the zodiac

Every 2.5 days, the Moon moves into a new zodiac sign. This means that in every 28.5-day cycle, she visits each zodiac sign once.

Each zodiac sign brings its own influences and energies, so it's worth taking notice of which sign she's in at any given time.

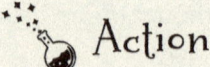

Action

From this moment, start noticing what phase the Moon is in and how the energies affect you physically, emotionally and mentally.

Chapter 3: Cycles

Weekly cycles - sacred days

Each day has its own unique energies, which are influenced by the planets. This makes it easy to utilise these energies either personally or when you're doing magickal work.

Have you noticed that your energy ebbs and flows throughout the day, or that you feel more tired on some days than on others? Maybe you've also noticed that things seem to work out better on some days, but not so much on others?

Imagine being so in tune with the natural energy flows of each day that you can plan out your activities and tasks to your best advantage. Imagine easily manifesting your desires. Then imagine actually managing your own energy so that you're buzzing all day and resting when you need to.

It would be amazing, right?

Let's have a closer look at how we can do just that, day by day.

Sunday - sacred to the Sun

Use the power of the Sun to:

- add oomph to new ventures
- bring an end to a period of poverty and bad luck
- enable you to connect with and strengthen your own identity
- facilitate change and transformation
- help increase your vitality and life force
- increase your ability to attract wealth and prosperity.

Monday - sacred to the Moon

Use the magick of the Moon to:

- bring more harmony to your family, or work at reconciliation
- connect with animals

- explore women's mysteries and the Divine Feminine
- increase fertility
- gain clarity around the rhythms of your body
- perform herb magic
- practise your divination
- release emotional issues
- understand your dreams
- work with the tides and the element of water.

Tuesday – sacred to Mars

Mars is associated with the warrior god of Rome and, as such, represents anger, aggression, ambition and competitiveness. While these qualities might normally seem negative, you can use them for good on this day. For example, you can use Mars energy when you need strength or power to:

- defeat your enemies
- empower your health and vitality
- fight an injustice or protect your loved ones
- increase your passion and sex life
- overcome an exceedingly challenging situation.

Mars is also the god of agriculture, so you can ask for aid in bringing vitality and health to your crops or garden.

Wednesday – sacred to Mercury

Use Mercury energy for:

- boosting your luck
- matters involving communication, finance and commerce
- deterring a trickster or thief
- divination
- planning or booking travel
- setting boundaries.

Chapter 3: Cycles

Thursday – sacred to Jupiter

Thursday is a good day to focus on:

- attracting money, wealth, good luck and success
- banishing greed and wastefulness
- encouraging fidelity and loyalty in your relationship
- healing and regeneration, especially of your liver or circulatory system
- increasing anything, eg. love, happiness, influence, leadership skills, money or your career
- promoting justice and helping the law be on your side
- strengthening your faith in your spiritual journey
- studying and learning.

Just a caution: Jupiter energy can sometimes lead to excessive behaviour. However, being aware of this in any magick you perform can also help you to curb it if you need to.

Friday – sacred to Venus

Friday is associated with Venus and, therefore, with love and all love magick. On this day, focus on invoking the energies of love and beauty and use them to:

- attract prosperity
- bring pleasure in all its forms
- enhance your sex life, increase your (or your partner's) desire or seduce someone
- enhance your personal growth
- ensure victory
- improve relationships and bring harmony to your life or home
- increase fertility.

Saturday – sacred to Saturn

Saturn is associated with the principles of:

- boundaries
- limitation
- practicality
- reality
- restriction
- structure.

This energy can act as the face of reality, showing you the constraints of fate, time and space.

As such, Saturday is an ideal day to work on goal-setting for long-term projects. You can utilise this Saturn energy to transform challenges into opportunities *if* you're willing to put in the work and be patient.

Saturn also rules:

- agriculture
- generation
- liberation
- plenty
- dissolution
- time
- wealth.

You may therefore wish to invoke him when you perform any magick or personal tasks related to these areas.

Chapter 3: Cycles

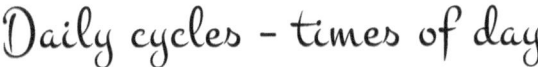

Daily cycles - times of day

In the same way that certain energies are present on different days, they're also present at different times of day. This is because Sun energy, which is more powerful and intense than Moon energy, waxes and wanes during the day.

There are four main times during each day when it's best to utilise the Sun's energy: sunrise, midday, sunset and midnight.

Sunrise

The Sun's energy is building at this time.

Suggestions

- Get up early and greet the Sun.
- Set your intentions for the day.
- Do a morning ritual, or get your exercise for the day done.
- Get your house chores out of the way.
- Do your meal prep.
- Start the day with a hot lemon water to flush out your system.
- Choose an oracle card for guidance.
- Start something new.
- Cleanse yourself and your home.

Midday

The energies at this time are similar to the Full Moon's, but more intense – like a burst.

Suggestions

If you have something big you're working on, like a work or house project, this is the best time to focus on it for maximum results. You could also:

- Manifest anything quickly, eg. money, strength or clarity.
- Move your body/exercise.
- Work on your creative project.
- Send distance healing to someone who needs it.
- Charge your crystals or magickal tools.

> ### Handy tip
> Remember to refuel your body with a nutritious meal after midday to keep the energy flowing beyond the burst.

Sunset

Energies are waning at sunset, so it's a good time to start wrapping things up for the day.

Suggestions

- Finish up anything you're working on for the day.
- Get dinner on early and eat early, so your food has time to digest.
- Rinse off any stresses from the day and let them go.
- Cleanse yourself with sage if those stresses are staying with you.
- Heal any pain you're experiencing.

This is also a good time to release and banish anything that's no longer serving you, rest and let your body heal.

Chapter 3: Cycles

If you still have a lot to achieve at this time of day, make sure you have a healthy mid-afternoon snack to sustain you and keep your energy up. However, try as well to simplify your daily routine, so you can align with the natural flow of the energy at this time.

Midnight

Just before midnight, the Sun's energy is at its lowest. After this point, the energies will start to build again.

Suggestions

- Sleeping is good! Let your body rest and rejuvenate.
- Journal out anything you're holding onto.
- Meditate.
- Light a candle, focus on it and release anything you can't let go of.
- Do some shadow work.
- Make contact with your ancestors or loved ones who've passed.
- Do a body scan and release any pain that's keeping you awake.

Your cycles

How does your body tune in to the cycles of Nature?

Because we're all a part of the Universe, it's only natural for our bodies to sync with Nature, both consciously and unconsciously. Have you ever noticed your moods changing with the Moon? Are there times of day when your energy feels low? Do you feel a little melancholy and reflective in winter, and bright with lots of energy in summer (unless you're like me – read my story below)?

In today's society, most people wouldn't have a clue about the answers to those questions. So many of us just run through each day from one task to another. We barely have enough time to breathe, let alone wonder whether our crappy mood is due to what the planets are doing!

But everyone's affected by Nature's energies — whether they know it or not.

A few examples...

- Women's menstrual cycles often align with the Moon's cycles and with those of other women they're close to or live with.
- We naturally feel drawn to different foods throughout the year.
- We need warmth, nourishment and water from Nature to live, and the ease with which we can obtain these things changes as the seasons do.
- Both the Moon's phases and the Sun's solar flares can affect our moods — quite dramatically for some people.
- Our energy levels can ebb and flow throughout the day, just like Nature's do.
- Some people feel the need to hibernate to cope with the season. Lots of people like to hibernate in winter to escape the cold. Or, if you're like me, you may prefer to hibernate in summer to escape the heat.
- Many people experience creative ups and downs as Nature's energies change. I'm more creative in summer and when the Moon is waxing, for example.
- It's common to feel either really emotional or emotionless at certain times of the day. For example, some people feel either really snarky or like a zombie first thing in the morning and then come alive after lunch. Meanwhile, others may be full of energy first thing, but get tired later in the day.

Chapter 3: Cycles

The key to understanding how this all affects you, and how to better tune in to these energies, is to observe and become aware of your own cycles. If you don't already, start paying close attention to:

- your moods
- your emotions
- your energy
- your habits throughout each day.

Case study: working with your own personal cycles

Now I'm going to turn everything I've just said on its head a little bit...

I'm a creature of opposites... I love the cold and don't function well at all in the heat. It's very hot in summer where I live. This means I find it difficult to cope with everyday tasks such as housework, cooking, going out or anything that involves too much physical activity.

For too long, though, I said yes to things I didn't want to do in summer because I thought I was 'supposed' to do them. I refused to honour what my mind, body and spirit really needed. All that brought me was unhappiness, which lowered my vibration. It was no fun.

Now I've learnt (finally) that it's imperative for my mental wellbeing to do what I can to flow with each season while still honouring my own needs.

So, as with the other seasons, I honour what's sacred to summer and the changes this season brings. I eat summer food and I drink summer drinks. I create a lot and spend lots of time outside (in the pool!) too. Plus, I use the Sun's energy in my magick.

However, to live more in tune with my own flow, I also:

- hibernate in summer instead of winter
- use my slow cooker a bit in summer, so I can put a meal on in the cool of the morning and avoid my hot kitchen later on
- reflect on the year that has been, journal a lot, and put all my plans/goals for the year into place
- focus more on my face-to-face business clients, and schedule all my big away-from-home events between autumn and the end of spring.

I share this because it's important to know that it's OK if you don't align with the traditional attributes of the seasons or Moon phases! You can still observe the gifts of each, use the energies and pay homage in whatever way feels best to you.

But, at the same time, you need to flow with whatever way your mind, body and soul are asking you for as well. Don't resist your natural urges!

Esbats

An esbat is either a Moon ceremony or a time to celebrate Full Moon rituals. As we discussed earlier in the chapter, the Full Moon is when Moon energy peaks, so it's an excellent time to do magick of any kind.

It's also a good time to stock up on supplies that you'll need for the month ahead. And it's an excellent time to plan celebrations like dedications and initiations or naming ceremonies. That's why, in the ritual below, you'll harness the Full Moon's power to dedicate yourself to your magick.

When you plan an esbat, don't forget to note which sign of the zodiac the Moon is in. Remember that each zodiac sign brings with it different influences, so ensure those influences align with your ritual.

Chapter 3: Cycles

Your ritual work: a Full Moon esbat

Intention

Dedication to your magick.

Timing

The Full Moon, after dark.

You will need

- A white altar cloth.
- A white candle.
- A red and a green candle (or other God/Goddess representations).
- White flowers.
- A moonstone crystal or other crystal sacred to the Moon (see Appendix C).
- A piece of paper and a pen.
- Something to symbolise your dedication: this could be anything – perhaps a sacred crystal or piece of jewellery, or a Moon statue or ornament.
- Rock salt.
- All the items you need to cast your basic circle from Chapter 2 (salt, water, smudge stick, etc.)

Ritual steps

1. Gather the tools you'll need and place them on or around your altar.
2. Have a cleansing wash/shower, and – using the rock salt mixed with a little water to make a paste – scrub all over your body to purify yourself.

3. Hop out and towel yourself dry. Don't put any products on your body at this point – you want to perform this ritual in as natural a state as possible.
4. Go to your altar and use your smudge stick to cleanse yourself, your space and all the items you'll use for your ritual.
5. Cast a simple circle as you did in Chapter 2.
6. If you haven't done so already, dress your altar with the flowers, crystal and anything else you've chosen to include.
7. Take a few moments to meditate on your intention for this ritual: dedicating yourself to your magickal practice. Ask yourself:

    - What does this mean to you?
    - How important is it?
    - Will it become a part of your daily life?
    - What sacred promises will you make to yourself and the Divine?

8. Take the piece of paper and pen and write down your dedication. Be as detailed as you like.
9. Speak whatever words you've written out loud to yourself. Then speak the words out loud again to the Universe. Finally, speak the words for the third time into your sacred object (your breath will empower it).
10. Sit for a few more moments in quiet contemplation, letting your dedication sink into your bones.
11. Journal your experience if you feel moved to.
12. Close the circle as described in Chapter 2 and snuff out your candle.
13. Keep your dedicated sacred object with you at all times. Recharge it with the words of your dedication whenever you feel the need to reconnect.
14. From this day forward, do something that nurtures your magickal craft every day.

Chapter 3: Cycles

How to integrate these teachings into your wholistic lifestyle

- 🧹 **Tune in: what season are you currently in?** Take note of:
    - what's happening in Nature
    - how you feel (eg. hot or cold)
    - what foods you're naturally being drawn to eat
    - how animals around you are behaving
    - how your energy feels.
- 🧹 **What phase is the Moon in, and how does that affect you physically, emotionally and mentally?** Is there anywhere in your life you might need to amp things up or slow things down? If the Moon is dark, for example, it's traditionally a good time to rest and regenerate.
- 🧹 **Revisit your upcoming plans and see how Nature's energies could possibly affect them.** For example:
    - if you're planning a business event, schedule it according to the Moon phase to give it the best chance of success
    - if you have an issue involving the law or the government, tend to it on a Thursday
    - if you need to reconnect with your love, schedule a date for a Friday.
- 🧹 **Start noticing how you feel at different times of the day.** Once you're aware of which times are best for you, start planning accordingly. For example, if you're starting something new, you might give it a positive boost with dawn energy.
- 🧹 **Plan a simple ritual.** As you plan, take all of Nature's cycles into account – the season, Moon phase, day and time of day.
- 🧹 **Start living more in alignment with the season you're in.** Just like in the quote I shared earlier in the chapter, eat the food and drink the drink.

- Take note of your own body's cycles and see how they align with the Moon's. Once you understand how your body tunes in to the Moon, you can start living more harmoniously with her natural energies.

Book of Shadows

- Record information about the Moon, seasons and days.
- Record your dedication ritual.

Journal tasks

- Journal your observations from your ritual.
- Open your awareness and start journalling about your cycles: your moods, your emotions, your energy and your habits. How do your own cycles fit in with those of Nature?
- Note too the phase and zodiac sign that the Moon is in, and the time of day and season.

In time, you'll begin to see a pattern. Once you identify this pattern, you can start to align yourself more with it, which will enhance your wholistic lifestyle.

Chapter 3: Cycles

Summary – Chapter 3

- 🧹 Everything in Nature is cyclic.
- 🧹 Externally, we can see these cycles taking place yearly, monthly, weekly and even daily.
- 🧹 Our bodies and internal cycles will naturally tune in to Nature's cycles – the seasons, Moon phases and the times of day.
- 🧹 As Nature's cycles change, so too do the energies – and it's important to tune in and flow with those energies to harness them.

CHAPTER 4
Elemental Magick

The elements

The elements of Earth, Air, Fire and Water are physical manifestations of Nature, while Aether or Spirit is of the celestial realm. Each element relates to a direction – respectively North, South, East, West and Centre. Each embodies its own qualities and energies that you can use to benefit both your daily life and your magick.

> The elements of Earth, Air, Fire and Water are physical manifestations of Nature, while Aether or Spirit is of the celestial realm.

When you feel into the qualities of each element, you can experience its energy – and that energy can then greatly enhance your rituals. For example, if you need something to happen quickly, use the element of Fire or Air to give your spell a burst of energy. On the other hand, if you need something to manifest slowly, use the element of Earth with its slower growth and transformative qualities.

How to work with the elements

Tuning in to and using these energies in your daily life can be as simple as invoking the element or energy you need whenever you need it. You could:

- invoke them when you're creating daily magick, like in your kitchen
- connect with each element's associated magickal beings
- use the power of each element to cleanse and heal you.

An example of this in action is honouring all the elements when you're working in your garden. When you're planting something new or tending your plants, be sure to bless each of them with all of the elements. Call on Earth and Water to nurture and nourish your plants, Fire to accelerate their growth and Air to give them the breath of life.

You'll find more specific ways to work with each element in the next sections of this chapter.

Spend time connecting with each element

It's important to connect with the elements and show them due respect and reverence before you start to work with them in elemental magick.

I'd suggest intentionally spending time in Nature with each of them to connect with them and experience for yourself how their energies feel. As you tune in to each one, you'll get a better sense of how to work with it.

> ### ✨ Handy tip
>
> I regularly feel a physical and spiritual pull to head to the beach and soak up the energy of the elements. I connect with Fire from the Sun, Water the from the ocean, Earth from the sand and Air from the wind.
>
> I always leave feeling calmer, clearer, grounded and more connected to the Divine.

To help you start getting to know each element, I've compiled a list of associations based on my own observations. May it inspire you and help you to gain an understanding of how each element's energies work.

Chapter 4: Elemental Magick

The magick of Earth

When I feel into Earth, I think of strength, stability and support. I also think of nourishment and regeneration, and I feel ancient wisdom and power. So these energies would be wonderful for any work involving healing, grounding, growth or transformation.

> When I feel into Earth, I think of strength, stability and support.

Direction: North.

Attributes: deep, energising, grounding, healing, nurturing, nourishing, safe, solid, strong, supportive, transformative, warm.

Energy: depth, fertility, regeneration and rebirth, stability, wisdom.

Colours: black, brown, grey, green, orange, red, yellow.

Crystals: aragonite, black obsidian, black onyx, emerald, hematite, jasper, jet, malachite, peridot, petrified wood, quartz.

Goddesses: Ceres, Cybele, Demeter, Eostre, Gaia, Joro, Nerthus, Pomona, Persephone, Prithvi, Rhea.

Gods: Arawn, Athos, Cernunnos, Dionysis, Geb, Pan.

Magickal Beings: gnomes, fairies, elves.

Perform Earth rituals for

- balance
- binding
- building solid foundations in your life
- connecting deeply with our mother (Nature)
- divination – especially using tools of Earth, such as crystals

- growing things in your life – for example, projects or relationships
- planting seeds – for example, new ventures, new creations or new beginnings
- reconnecting with yourself – coming 'home'
- releasing things that no longer serve you (bury them for Mother Earth to transform)
- success and money spells
- transformation.

Invoke Earth in your daily life to

- bring stability to your day/life
- connect with your inner kitchen witch
- ground and centre yourself (especially if you have a busy day ahead)
- help to nurture yourself through transformation
- stay connected to your Self.

Practical applications

- Burn or make your own earthy incense.
- Cook earthy root vegetables when you need grounding.
- Harvest herbs and flowers from your garden and add to your cooking to use in kitchen witchery.
- Make clay statues.
- Make herbal sachets for rituals and healing.
- Plant your garden.
- Use or make your own magick salts or bath salts.

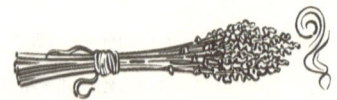

Chapter 4: Elemental Magick

The magick of Air

When I tune in to the element of Air, I feel flow, change, gentleness, strength and life. Working with Air is wonderful for both gentle and dramatic change, as well as for connecting with your body through your breath, moving energy and experiencing freedom.

> When I tune in to the element of Air, I feel flow, change, gentleness, strength and life.

Direction: East.

Attributes: breath, change, communication, freedom, flow, intellect, life.

Energy: boosting, gentle movement, revitalising, resisting, twirling, whirling.

Colours: blue, crimson, silver, white, yellow.

Crystals: amethyst, blue calcite, citrine, gold beryl, lapis lazuli, sapphire, smoky quartz, topaz, yellow jasper.

Goddesses: Arianrhod, Aradia, Aura, Nuit, Oya, Urania.

Gods: Anemoi (Greek god of wind), Enlil, Odin, Shu, Thoth.

Magickal Beings: faeries.

Perform Air rituals for

- breathing life into yourself or into a project
- bringing swift change
- connecting with your bird totem
- clearing clutter from your schedule and allowing more freedom, or clearing resistance
- communication and expressing yourself
- developing your psychic powers

- gaining clarity, or learning and gaining knowledge
- shaking things up and moving stagnant energy
- travel.

Invoke Air in your daily life to

- approach things more gently
- bring things to a swift close or, alternatively, slow them down
- clear stagnant energy around your home, or clear your head
- communicate clearly and express yourself better
- flow through your day with more ease.

Practical applications

- Make and burn incense to represent Air.
- Hang crystals or wind chimes in the breeze to change energy.
- Meditate.
- Perform weather magick.
- Use your breath to empower objects like crystals.
- Use bells or a singing bowl, either in ritual or to move energy in stagnant areas of your home.

The magick of Fire

For me, Fire energy is incredibly sacred (maybe because I'm a fire sign). It's something that sustains life but also takes it away, then heals and regenerates. Fire is therefore transformative, often in a fast, explosive way. This means Fire magick is good when you need some oomph or a burst of power to get things moving quickly. For example, it's perfect for transformational work if you've been stagnant.

> Fire energy is incredibly sacred: it sustains life but also takes it away, then heals and regenerates.

Chapter 4: Elemental Magick

Direction: South.

Attributes: boosting, cleansing, clearing, creating, destroying, energising, strengthening, transforming.

Energy: angry, creative, enthusiastic, fast, hot, passionate, powerful, smouldering, uncontainable, unpredictable, wild.

Colours: crimson, gold, orange, red, white, yellow.

Crystals: carnelian, amber, ruby, garnet, fire opal, onyx, sunstone.

Goddesses: Brigid, Chantico, Hestia, Kali, Pele, Sekhmet, Vesta.

Gods: Hephaestus, Kagu-tsuchi, Ogun, Ra, Vulcan.

Magickal Beings: salamanders.

Perform Fire rituals for

- adding 'fire' to your sex life
- connecting with your ancestors
- creating something new
- giving a boost to a project
- healing
- love and lust
- purification
- recreating yourself
- releasing and banishing.

Invoke Fire in your daily life to

- add zest and passion to your love trysts
- bring fire to your creativity
- 'fire up' your motivation
- get a quick energy boost
- speed up or boost your transformation.

Practical applications

- 🧹 Burn things you want to banish.
- 🧹 Cook with magick – for example, add some chilli to your dish to fire up your energy.
- 🧹 Heat potions.
- 🧹 Melt wax to unseal and seal things or to inscribe during spellwork.
- 🧹 Perform candle magick. This can be as simple as lighting a candle to set an intention or create an energy, or it can mean using a candle within a full ritual.

The magick of Water

When I tune in to Water, I feel the energies of cooling, healing, cleansing and flowing. Water can be so gentle and calming, but also strong, unpredictable and destructive. As with all the elements, I have a very healthy respect for Water. I love how it calms and balances me, but I also appreciate its power whenever I'm near a waterfall or a raging torrent. I love communing with Water when I cast spells for purification, releasing or transformation.

> When I tune in to Water, I feel the energies of cooling, healing, cleansing and flowing.

Direction: West.

Attributes: change, fluidity, harmony, healing, life force, release, surrender, transformation, wisdom.

Energy: changing, cleansing, emotional, flexible, flowing, nurturing, peaceful, rushing, supportive, wild, unpredictable.

Colours: aqua, blue, green, grey, navy, turquoise, white.

Crystals: amethyst, aquamarine, blue lace agate, blue tourmaline, pearl, sapphire, topaz.

Chapter 4: Elemental Magick

Goddesses: Aphrodite, Danu, Doris, Mazu, Oshun, Sedna.

Gods: Aegaeon, Freyr, Lir, Poseidon, Susanoo, Tangaroa, Triton.

Magickal Beings: mermaids, water sprites.

Perform Water rituals for

- bringing more flow to your life
- cleansing and purifying
- creating peace and reconciliation
- divination and understanding your dreams
- healing – both emotional and physical
- love and relationships
- protection
- releasing resistance to change
- washing away whatever no longer serves you.

Invoke Water in your daily life to

- cleanse and purify
- flow with more ease and grace through your day, or flow through change
- heal
- invoke love
- reconcile peacefully
- release emotion.

Practical applications

- Create a cleansing bath.
- Make beauty products.
- Make holy water by charging ordinary water under the Full Moon, or by asking the God or Goddess to bless it.
- Make potions, tonics and tinctures.
- Use in blessing rituals.

The magick of Aether or Spirit

Although we're covering it last, the element of Aether/Spirit is the first of the five elements. It exists within all the other elements and is known as the most subtle. In fact, 'Aether' translates to 'emptiness'. So when I tune in to Aether/Spirit, I feel immense peace, lightness and freedom. It's the one energy that lets me quiet my mind – a very difficult thing for me to do. I also think of this space as a kind of incubator. It's somewhere ideas, dreams and divine downloads sit before they become things of substance. If you feel creatively stuck or stagnant, or your mind is clogged up and clarity is hard to find, try to connect with Spirit and let go...

> When I tune in to Aether/Spirit, I feel immense peace, lightness and freedom.

Direction: None.

Attributes: divine intelligence, energy in motion, eternity, pure essence – it's believed that Aether is what the Gods breathe, transmutation.

Aether also helps you to connect with more than one element at a time to bring balance and helps you to connect to the Wheel of the Year and magickal tools.

Energy: authenticity, freedom, incubation, limitlessness, movement, mystery, spaciousness, subtleness, weightlessness.

Colours: black, white and rainbow.

Crystals: angel aura, meteorite, quartz, zebra stone.

Goddesses: Amaterasu, Cerridwen, Diana, Fortuna, Gaia, Hathor, Hestia, Inanna, Isis.

Gods: Apollo, Baal, Odin, Shiva, Tyr.

Magickal Beings: None.

Chapter 4: Elemental Magick

Perform Aether rituals for

- change and transformation
- connecting with the spirit world
- creating an illusion, or creation generally
- divination
- gaining guidance and direction.

Invoke Aether in your daily life to

- commune more easily with spirits
- flow through change more easily
- stay focused.

Practical applications

- Alchemy.
- Clearing your mind.
- Prayer.
- Meditation.

Your ritual work: honouring the elements

Intention

To connect with and honour the elements.

Timing

Any.

You will need

- Four white candles to mark the directions.
- Something to mark out your circle with, eg. stones, chalk or salt (optional).

- A smudge stick.
- A lighter.
- Core representations of each element – a bowl of water for Water, incense for Air, a candle for Fire and a bowl of salt or earth for Earth.
- Other representations of each element (optional) – for example, coloured candles, crystals, Tarot cards, trinkets/symbols, plants or flowers or a coloured cloth.

Ritual steps

1. Gather the tools you'll need.
2. Find a space outdoors to conduct your ritual. This should be somewhere private where you won't be disturbed.
3. Mark out your circle. You might like to use stones, chalk or salt for this. Make it at least nine feet in diameter, although I'd suggest a little bigger for this exercise.
4. Create five separate altars within your circle. Create one for each of the directions (North, South, East and West) and one in the centre for Spirit.

   Note: these altars don't need to be fancy. You can just put your representations of each element on the ground if you prefer. However, take your time with this part so that what you create feels good to you.
5. Use the smudge stick to cleanse yourself, your circle and all the items you'll use for your ritual.
6. Cast the simple circle as you learnt in Chapter 2, leaving out the part about the elements.
7. Sit in the centre of the circle and take a few moments to meditate on your intention for this ritual: connecting with the elements.
8. Stand up and walk around the circle to each of the altars, starting in the North. Light each element's candle, sit before its altar and pay homage to it in whatever way feels right to you.

Chapter 4: Elemental Magick

Be aware that there's no right or wrong in this ritual. You could just say something simple like, "I honour you, Earth." You could meditate on each element's qualities. Or, alternatively, you could make an elaborate speech dedicating yourself to each element if that feels good to you.

However you pay homage, finish at the Spirit altar.

9. When you're finished, spend a few minutes simply feeling into the connection you've just made.
10. Finally, close circle in the usual way (see Chapter 2).

How to integrate these teachings into your wholistic lifestyle

- **Begin by spending time outdoors as often as possible.** As you do, feel into each element – first physically and then intuitively. Touch your bare feet to the Earth, feel the wind on your face, experience the fire of the Sun on your skin and swish your fingers or toes through water. Notice any feelings, thoughts, messages or insights.

- **When collecting anything from Nature, ask permission first as a show of respect.** Then pause to listen for the answer. For example, I recently needed an offering for a public ritual I was attending and I saw some pretty purple flowers in a public garden bed.

  I asked permission before I picked any and listened for the answer. I got a clear no from some flowers that looked like they had a bit more growing to do and a yes from other plants that were flourishing.

- **Welcome the energy of the elements into your rituals.** I like to bid each element welcome while I hold a representation of it, and then I ask it to witness/stand sentinel during my working.

Wholistic Witchcraft

- 🧙 **Speak to the elements and give them your thanks.** Honour them and show them your respect, so they'll be more inclined to work with you. I do this whenever I'm outside connecting with Nature and also during rituals.
- 🧙 **Invoke the elements when you need them in your daily life and your rituals.** For example, invoke Water for cleansing, Earth for grounding, Fire for energy and Air for flow.
- 🧙 **Make little altars out in Nature to honour each element.** Use representations of each element from Nature itself (but, as above, ask permission first).
- 🧙 **Invoke the elements when you practise kitchen witchery.** Try blessing the water you'll cook in, or add the fire of chillies to your dish for energy, for example.
- 🧙 **Honour the elements in your garden by leaving them offerings.** Go with whatever intuitively feels right here, and ask them to bless your plants with health and growth.
- 🧙 **Spend time outside near the water when your vibe is low to connect with all the elements in one place.** You could go to a beach as I mentioned that I like to do, or head to a stream or lake. The combination of all the elemental energies brings balance and healing to you mentally, physically and spiritually.

Book of Shadows

☽ Record the elemental information and associations.

☽ Record your ritual and anything you notice.

Chapter 4: Elemental Magick

> ### Journal tasks
>
> 🧹 Spend some time in Nature, exploring each of the elements.
>
> 🧹 Really feel into each element, and then journal your feelings/observations.

Summary - Chapter 4

- 🧹 The elements are physical manifestations of Nature.
- 🧹 In my practice, I connect most with Earth, Air, Water and Fire, and sometimes Aether/Spirit.
- 🧹 Connecting with these elements and bringing their energies into your ritual and daily life can enhance and empower both.
- 🧹 Being out in Nature is the best way to connect with each element.
- 🧹 Pay attention to the associations that are connected to each element so you can use them as representations in your rituals.

CHAPTER 5

Deities and Magickal Beings

Deities

What are deities?

Deities are divine beings who are identified as gods and goddesses in polytheistic religions. 'Polytheistic' is Greek for 'many gods' – and the term describes any religion that worships or believes in multiple gods, such as many schools of Paganism or Witchcraft, Hinduism and Chinese Buddhism, to name a few.

> Deities are divine beings who are identified as gods and goddesses in polytheistic religions.

Some religions and cultures believe in just one supreme being, which is known as monotheism (Greek for 'one god'). Most others, however, are polytheistic, believing in many gods and goddesses. In polytheistic religions, each god or goddess has their own attributes and gifts. Each deity is also part of a complex hierarchy within their overall pantheon (all the deities of a particular culture).

According to many texts I've read, however, all gods are ultimately one god, and all goddesses are ultimately one goddess. This is what I've come to believe myself.

Why work with deities?

Deity is embodied in all living things. While some religions build special temples for their gods, Witches and Pagans know they can honour and connect with the Divine anywhere. When you're worshipping the beauty in Nature, connecting with your animal totems or summoning magickal beings, you're connecting with Deity.

My connection to the Divine continues to be one of the most important parts of my spiritual practice. No matter what's happening in my life, I always feel supported, loved and connected to their presence. They're an integral part of my spiritual 'team of advisers' and guides.

To strengthen your connection to the Divine, pray to your chosen deities, call them into your rituals or ask for their guidance throughout your day. You'll benefit from feeling supported, guided and empowered, both magickally and in your daily life.

> ### Handy tip
>
> Because I believe that all gods are one god and all goddesses are one goddess, when I cast a circle, I usually invoke 'the Goddess and God' to protect and bless it.
>
> Sometimes, however, I'll call on specific deities that are associated with particular qualities or gifts, as I mention in the following list.

Specific deities

In Appendix D, you'll find a comprehensive list of gods and goddesses. However, I'd highly recommend researching further to really get to know any gods or goddesses you're drawn to as part of expanding your magickal knowledge. As a starting point for this research, you'll find a list of books that I recommend and love in Appendix I.

Chapter 5: Deities and Magickal Beings

In the meantime, here's just a teensy selection of deities that I personally like to work with as examples. (You might notice that they're all female, which is purely because they're the ones who resonate with me most. I *have* worked with male deities, but only occasionally.)

> I'd highly recommend researching further to really get to know any gods or goddesses you're drawn to, as part of expanding your magickal knowledge.

- **Aphrodite:** *Greek goddess of love.* I work with Aphrodite all the time in love and beauty spells.
- **Brigid:** *Celtic goddess of creativity.* I work with Brigid in meditations and spells when I need inspiration and a boost of creativity. (And yes, I invoked her a LOT while I was writing this book!)
- **Demeter:** *Greek goddess of the harvest.* Demeter is one of my matron goddesses, and I work with her for her mothering and nurturing energy. I think of her as a mentor, protector and guide.
- **Hecate:** *Greek goddess of witchcraft, magick, crossroads and the night.* I've worked a lot with Hecate in shadow journeys and meditations when I'm seeking guidance about which path to take.
- **Hestia:** *Greek goddess of hearth and home.* I invoke Hestia all the time when I'm in the kitchen creating for family and friends, or when I need to bring more harmony into my home.
- **Kali:** *Hindu goddess of creation/destruction.* Kali is another of my matron goddesses, and I (mainly) work with her when I'm casting protection spells.
- **Lakshmi:** *Hindu goddess of abundance.* I work with Lakshmi for prosperity and abundance meditations and spells.
- **Lilith:** *Mesopotamian goddess of power.* I work with Lilith in empowerment spells – she helps me to reclaim my power and wholly step into it.

- **Minerva:** *Roman goddess of wisdom and beliefs.* I work with Minerva a fair bit in meditations and healing work.
- **The Morrigan:** *Irish triple goddess of war and fate.* The Morrigan is also the goddess of death and transformation, and I worked with her when I was undergoing intense transformational ritual journeys.

How to work with deities

To consciously connect with a deity, it's important to educate yourself about them. You need to understand their history and the myths surrounding them to truly understand why they're connected to certain energies and associations.

Once you know this, you can begin to build a relationship with the deities you resonate with most. The best way to do this is by honouring them and showing your respect. Making an offering to them is a great way to begin. Once you've felt a connection, you can start having a conversation with them, praying to them and connecting with their particular energy.

Then, when you feel comfortable, you can begin to invoke them in your rituals and ask for their blessings whenever you need them.

My favourite ways to do this are either sitting at my altar in a focused ritual or being out in Nature, where I can feel their presence everywhere. To align more with the wholistic practices we've talked about in the book, I recommend doing both.

Following are other methods I often use:

- **Speak to them and ask them to bless me with particular attributes.** These might include clarity or compassion, for example. I most often do this through ritual, but also sometimes spontaneously when I'm just going about my day.

Chapter 5: Deities and Magickal Beings

For example, when I realise I need a good dose of courage, I might call on Mars or Ares. Or, when I'm out in Nature, I'll speak to them out loud to honour them.

- **Place items associated with a particular deity on my altar to honour them, then ask them to bless my ritual.** For example, I might use coins as a representation of Lakshmi to honour her if I'm casting an abundance and prosperity spell. I'll often use a god or goddess Tarot card to represent them on my altar too.
- **Ask them to bless and consecrate any magickal items I make.** These might include incense or wands, for example.

Magickal beings

What are magickal beings?

Magickal beings aren't deities as such, but they're also not mortal. I've read them described as 'minor deities' or 'spirits' that dwell in other realms, which I've come to know as the Otherworld.

> Magickal beings aren't deities as such, but they're also not mortal.

At times, magickal beings gift us with their energy in our realm. This means we can work with them and honour them as we do with deities. Some people are lucky enough to actually see magickal beings or representations of them – for example, a coloured bubble or shape. However, most people experience them simply as an energy.

I'm sure we've all read about magickal beings or watched movies in which they were important characters. Think of the fairy godmothers, dwarves and mermaids in fairy tales, and the elves, wizards and dragons in epic fantasy movies like *Lord of the Rings* or the *Narnia* series.

As a child (and into adulthood too), I always believed that these beings were real. After all, the stories had to come from somewhere, right?

Wholistic Witchcraft

While I've never been lucky enough to see a magickal being – or not consciously, anyhow – I know people who have. I also know of many other encounters across the world that have been documented for centuries, if not millennia.

Unfortunately, texts I've read say that as humans became more greedy and self-centred, the veils between the worlds thickened. Eventually, magickal beings were no longer free to travel between the dimensions as they once did. Perhaps they can only visit the earthly realm now at special times and in places of energetic significance.

I hope and believe that as the world and humanity 'awaken', we can build meaningful relationships with magickal beings once more. Perhaps we'll be able to work alongside them in a fuller capacity as we once did. We can each play our role and begin right now with some of the tips I've listed later in the chapter.

Why work with magickal beings?

Magickal beings can gift you with insight, knowledge, protection, magick and energy. Each one possesses their own special gifts and wisdom, which means they can be wonderful allies.

> Magickal beings can gift you with insight, knowledge, protection, magick and energy.

If you're lucky, a magickal being you work with may just share some of their magickal gifts with you. You may be able to use these gifts in your spellwork, in your garden, around your home or to protect your family.

As always, when you work with any beings from other realms, it's important to be mindful and respectful. The aim is to build and then enjoy a relationship of mutual trust with them.

Chapter 5: Deities and Magickal Beings

Types of magickal beings

Faeries and elves

These beings dwell on faery hills and in flower gardens, faery rings, wild places, forests and fields. They know the magickal secrets of herbs, stones and animals. They love to dance and play, and they can see the future.

However, they can be spiteful and tricksy at times, so take care when you work with them. Show them respect and offer them gifts, and they may share their secrets with you.

Gnomes

Gnomes can dwell within the Earth, within trees or around the roots of large trees. They often care for wild animals and tend to plants and trees.

They're gentle and quiet, and can be benevolent – rewarding you with happiness or offering you their protection. However, they're also known to be cantankerous if bothered or disrupted in their tasks, and they aren't afraid to deal out punishment, so take care.

Trolls and dwarves

These beings prefer caves, mines, areas under bridges, and in the hollows of hills. They have a deep knowledge of gems and metals – knowing where to find them, and how to forge and shape them.

They're often depicted as being grumpy, but they're also very strong, wise and loyal.

Brownies and kobolds

These beings of the Earth often live in human homes. Legend says that they like to help 'the lady of the house' with chores at night while everyone's asleep, while also protecting her family.

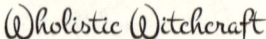

If you're kind, they'll be loyal to you and your home. Leaving milk and cookies out for them is always nice too.

Dragons

Dragons are the keepers of ancient wisdom and are strong protectors. They're often depicted as fearsome, fire-breathing creatures that only destroy but, while they can be fierce, they're so much more than that.

They're strong, resilient, courageous, wise, compassionate, protective and magickal beings. And despite being of the Earth itself, they embody all five of the elements within themselves.

Salamanders

These fire spirits are depicted as lizard-like creatures that live within a flame. They can be both creative and destructive, so take care when you work with them.

Invoke them when you do any rituals involving fire or passion, or when you need to bring a burst of energy to something.

Merpeople

Dwelling in the ocean, these half-human, half-fish beings are most often called mermaids. Tales about them vary. Some claim they lure men to their deaths and ships to their ruin, while in others, they help seafarers to safety.

In all tales, though, merpeople are beautiful, magickal beings that can be equally fierce and gentle. They love to sing beautiful melodies, play and delight in the Sun. They're passionate and embody grace, peace, beauty, creativity and magick.

Water sprites

These magickal beings live mostly in streams, creeks and brooks. They're often depicted as small beings with wings who can fly at times and can breathe both in and out of the water.

Chapter 5: Deities and Magickal Beings

They love to frolic and play as they flow with the natural currents. And in fact, this is one of their greatest gifts – teaching us how to flow with life and adapt to change just as currents do. They're mostly friendly unless they feel threatened, so always be kind and gentle with them.

How to work with magickal beings

Each of these beings has their own characteristics and energies, and you'll need to take these into account when you work with them. For example, as we mentioned above, some faeries can be tricksy or spiteful. You don't want them playing any tricks on you that could alter the course of your ritual!

Magickal beings are powerful and you need to respect them. Many have grown mistrustful of humans over the years due to ill treatment. Because of this, you need to make a genuine effort to connect with them and understand them.

> Magickal beings are powerful and you need to respect them.

Before you work with a magickal being, I strongly suggest taking time to research them. Then begin trying to build a relationship with them – much as you would with another human you want to be friends with. You could start by leaving them appropriate offerings and talking to them. Otherwise, they may well feel that your heart is in the wrong place and refuse to work with you.

Appropriate offerings

- flowers, fruits and shiny tokens for faeries
- flowers or shells for merpeople
- fresh organic foods like fruits, nuts, bread and honey for dwarves and gnomes
- jewels, crystals and gold coins for dragons
- milk and home-baked cookies for house brownies.

Ways to work with magickal beings

- 🧚 Ask brownies to protect you and your home.
- 🧚 Ask dragons to protect you and your home. You can also ask them for their wisdom or let them help you to connect with your ancestors and your roots.
- 🧚 Ask faeries to bless your garden or bless you with fertility – either for yourself or for things you need to bring to fruition.
- 🧚 Ask gnomes to help you connect with Mother Earth and also to heal trees on your property that might be ill.
- 🧚 Ask merpeople to protect you when you're travelling over the sea.

> To honour Deity and magickal beings, be respectful at all times. That means respecting them, yourself, others and Mother Earth.
>
> We must care for and nurture our magickal planet by treading on her as lightly as we can. It's our sacred duty to preserve what the gods have gifted us with and to protect life in all its forms.

Your ritual work: a dedication to the Goddess and God

Intention

In this ritual, you can dedicate yourself to the Goddess and God as a whole (working on the basis that all gods are one god).

Alternatively, you can choose specific deities that you particularly resonate with.

Chapter 5: Deities and Magickal Beings

Timing

Any.

You will need

- Four white candles to mark the directions.
- A red candle to represent the God and a green candle to represent the Goddess.
- A smudge stick.
- Other representations of the Goddess and God, or of the specific deity/deities you want to dedicate yourself to (optional). You can find deity associations for colours, crystals, animals and more in the Appendices to give you some ideas for these.
- Elemental representations – two bowls, each with salt and water, incense and one of the above candles.
- A lighter.

Ritual steps

1. Gather the tools you'll need.
2. Find a private space where you won't be disturbed – outdoors would be great for this one if possible. Set up your altar and ritual tools.
3. Use your smudge stick to cleanse yourself, your circle and all the items you'll use for your ritual.
4. Cast a simple circle as you did in Chapter 2.
5. Spend a few moments meditating on the Goddess and God or your specific deity/deities. Ask yourself:

    - What do they mean to you?
    - What's your connection with them?
    - How do they assist you in your daily life now?
    - How can you deepen your connection and relationship to them?

6. Now speak out loud to them, either offering them your blessings or dedicating yourself to them. Speak whatever words feel right to you that reflect the connection or relationship you wish to have with them.

   For example, I don't like to promise to 'serve' a deity. However, I do want to honour them greatly and work with them. The most important thing here is that you speak from the heart. You don't need to be fancy or eloquent – just be authentic.

7. Now spend a few moments feeling into the energetic bond and connection you've just made. Feel how it will positively impact you, both personally and magickally.

   Know that you can now call on your deity/deities or speak to them whenever you wish, and they'll always hear you.

8. Close circle in the usual way (see Chapter 2).

How to integrate these teachings into your wholistic lifestyle

- **The simplest way to connect with deities is to spend time outside.** The more you're present in Nature, the more you begin to understand that Deity is present in everything. Every tree, every plant, every living thing IS the Goddess and God in itself.
- **Read whatever you can on gods and goddesses.** In particular, read about any that you're keen to work with in your magick. Get to know them and their attributes. How can you bring their energy into your rituals?
- **Leave offerings for magickal beings in your garden and within your home.** See the list earlier in the chapter for ideas.
- **Place representations of the deities or magickal beings you wish to work with on your altar.** Again, see the Appendices for associations that will give you ideas of what to use for representations.

Chapter 5: Deities and Magickal Beings

- 🧙 **Talk to the deities you resonate with.** Pray to them, ask them for guidance, ask for their blessings and then look for signs that they've heard you. Keep your awareness open!

- 🧙 **Carry crystals that are associated with certain gods and goddesses on you to benefit from their energies.** For example, if you're seeking more love in your life, ask Aphrodite to bless a rose quartz crystal for you. Then carry it with you or keep it under your pillow.

- 🧙 **Ask the Goddess and God (or your chosen deity) to bless your magickal tools and cards.** You can do this when you first consecrate them, but also again each time you use them.

- 🧙 **Work with your crown chakra to activate and harmonise it.** This energy centre is your direct connection to the Divine.

Book of Shadows

☽ Record your ritual and observations.

☽ You might also like to record the information about magickal beings and deities. In particular, record how to honour and work with them.

Journal tasks

🧙 Journal your observations from your ritual work.

🧙 Also journal any experiences you've had with deities or magickal beings.

🧙 Journal about how you can connect with them now and how you'd like to work with them in the future.

Chapter 5: Deities and Magickal Beings

Summary - Chapter 5

- 🧹 Working with deities and magickal beings is an important part of wholistic witchcraft because it can open you to other energies, perspectives and wisdom.
- 🧹 Deities are divine beings, while magickal beings are minor deities or spirits that dwell within other realms.
- 🧹 Whichever beings you work with, it's important to learn as much as possible about them and treat them with respect to build a trusting relationship.
- 🧹 The best way to connect with deities and magickal beings is to be out in Nature.
- 🧹 Both deities and magickal beings have their own unique qualities and associations, so if you'd like to work with them, do your research first.

Section 2

Tools to Aid Your Journey

Now that she's understood and experienced energy and the cycles of Nature, the witchling has developed a sense of how she fits into this divine tapestry of life. Her awareness is growing. She's felt into what she now knows is her intuition, and begins tapping into it and allowing it to guide every step of her path.

Because she's become so closely connected to her environment, she begins to understand the importance of creating environments that nourish and protect her. She also understands how to ensure they give her a sacred space to dwell and be.

She realises though that her journey has only just begun, so she can only carry limited supplies. She creates impermanent spaces, which allow her to pack up the tools she's gathered on her travels and take them with her on a whim.

The twists and turns of her path now bring her into contact with other beings, both magickal and human. She begins to learn that she needn't travel this path alone. She can take travel companions along on the journey who'll teach, support and guide her as she continues to evolve personally and magickally.

This leg of her journey brings her enormous growth and sets her up for what's to come.

Welcome to Section 2, magickal one, and congratulations on how far you've come on your journey. Now that you've discovered more about yourself and how your world works energetically and cyclically, you can expand your awareness out. You can welcome in tools, practices and people that will help you continue to move forward on your path.

In this section, you'll learn about the ancient arts of divination and creating sacred spaces. These can enhance your daily experiences on both a personal and a magickal level. You'll also discover how to keep your magick with you at all times, whether you're at home, at work or away. This will help you to stay connected to your practice.

And, finally, you'll start to think about what I feel is one of the most important parts of any wholistic lifestyle – who you surround yourself with. The people in your circle can have a large influence on how empowered or disempowered you feel.

The knowledge and experience you gain from this section will be essential for the final part of your journey. At that point you'll dive deep, which means you'll need to feel supported and confident in your abilities.

So, by the end of this section, I want you to be ready to step into your truth and your power. Achieving this won't happen without its challenges, so the work you do now is so very important.

May you drink it all in, and allow this wisdom to support you moving forward.

Blessings

Bella x

CHAPTER 6

Divination

What is divination?

Divination is the art of using the energies of Nature, magickal tools and your own intuition to connect with the Divine to gain answers, clarity and guidance.

Humans have used divination since the beginning of time. Diviners have sought answers to questions through various means like reading signs, events or omens. They've also used divinatory tools that I'll discuss in depth later in this chapter.

> Divination is the art of using the energies of Nature, magickal tools and your own intuition to connect with the Divine to gain answers, clarity and guidance.

I find that divination is an extremely helpful tool when I need guidance, clarity, energy or answers. It often reassures me that I'm on the right path or tells me when I need to change course. Plus, it can also offer me insight into why something's happening or what might be coming up for me.

For these reasons, I believe that divination can be an extremely useful tool in both your personal and magickal journeys. If you haven't started to explore it already, I'd encourage you to begin now.

Types of divination

According to psychologist Julian James (2000), divination can fall into four categories:

- omens
- sortilege
- augury
- spontaneous.

Following is a very brief introduction to each category.

Omens

Omens are signs that can be either good or bad. They can be perceived as a stroke of either good or bad luck. They're often thought of as signs of whether a future event or situation that's specific to a person will turn out well or not.

For example: some people may see a crow flying across their path as an omen of death or ill health.

Sortilege (also known as cleromancy)

Sortilege involves casting or throwing 'lots' or 'sortes' of an object in order to read or decipher the signs from them. The sorte objects can be anything, but are most commonly sticks, stones, bones, beans or coins.

The reader deciphers the message by one of the following methods:

- **matching the pattern they observe to a predetermined result:** for example, they might decide before throwing the sortes that one pattern means 'yes' and another means 'no'.
- **intuitively interpreting the random pattern that results:** for example, they might notice the shape the sortes have fallen into or intuitively note where certain objects fall in relation to others.

Chapter 6: Divination

This practice dates back to ancient times, and you can use it for anything where you require an intuitive answer.

For example: you might use this practice to 'tell a fortune', to determine an important outcome or to find out what the will of the Divine is for you.

Augury

This is the practice of ranking a set of possibilities to divine the will of the gods. According to ancient texts, augury specifically refers to reading the behaviour patterns of birds. This practice was also called 'taking the auspices', and the more 'auspicious' something was, the more the gods were seen to favour it.

For example: an augur (reader) would designate one side of an area as meaning one answer and the other side as a second answer, then release a flock of birds. Whichever side the birds flew to would answer the proposed question.

Another method was to ask whether a given situation or course of action had the gods' favour. For example, the diviner might go out in Nature and wait for birds to appear. The number of birds would determine the answer – the more birds that appeared, the more auspicious the situation/action was seen to be.

Another type of augury was Haruspicy, which involved reading the entrails and body parts of animals. Diviners would look for irregularities in an organ, and note its colour and health. An animal's liver was the most valued organ, as it was known as the source of life. If a liver was healthy, the augur thought the gods were present in it – an auspicious sign.

Spontaneous

This is a free form of divination in which the diviner can use any medium they lay their eyes on.

For example: the reader may spontaneously use cards or rune stones by asking a question, then randomly choosing a card or stone and taking its message as their answer. Modern Feng Shui and reading auras are also forms of spontaneous divination.

Another common form of spontaneous divination is dowsing. This practice uses a Y-shaped stick or two L-shaped rods to locate objects like water, crystals, metal, oil, gravesites and ore. Although there's no science to back its accuracy (because it's scientifically inexplicable), intuition and random chance can work together to obtain a successful outcome.

The divination method I most often use is spontaneous: I'll randomly pick a card or a rune daily for general guidance.

Divination using tools

I use several tools to divine information in wholistic witchcraft. Below, you'll find a brief introduction to some of the more well-known tools that I use regularly.

> With any divination tool, your intuition is the number one factor in getting an accurate reading.

Entire books can be (and have been) written about each tool. So if there's one you're particularly interested in, I'd recommend researching it further by reading specialised books, searching online for information or studying with an expert.

General guidelines for divination tools

Please be aware that with any divination tool, your intuition is the number one factor in getting an accurate reading.

For example, when I do a Tarot reading, I always feel into the card first. I ask questions like:

- How do I feel when I connect with this card?
- What does the picture mean to me?
- What do the symbols, numbers or colours mean to me?

Chapter 6: Divination

I'll go with my intuition first, and only then – if I feel that I want to – refer to the book that accompanies my deck.

Additionally, before you use any divination tools, please cleanse them and attune them to you and your personal energy.

For example, I'll usually cleanse new cards with sage smoke, then leave them on my altar under the Full Moon's light before I use them. If I want to work deeply with a new set of cards, I'll often sleep with them beneath my pillow for a week or two to attune them to my energy.

Pendulums

A pendulum is a divinatory tool you can use to answer questions that have either a 'yes' or a 'no' answer.

Pendulums are usually made of crystal or stone. However, they can also be made of metal, and some people simply use a necklace with a charm on the bottom of it.

Whatever they're made of, pendulums are suspended by a chain that you hold onto so they can swing freely. They're also generally cylindrical with pointed tips and should be weighted to balance nicely and give an accurate reading.

To use: first, cleanse your pendulum with a smudge stick or cleansing incense, then attune it to you by holding it in your hand and allowing your energy to merge with it.

Next, say first "Yes" and then "No" out loud, noticing how the pendulum behaves in response to each statement. This behaviour will be different for each person. For example, *your* pendulum might move in a clockwise circle to signify 'yes' and side-to-side to signify 'no'.

Once you're clear on your pendulum's 'yes'/'no' movements, ask it a few questions that you already know the answers to. For example, you might ask, "Is the sky blue today?" This helps to make sure the pendulum is tuned into you and that it's giving you accurate answers.

When you feel that you and the pendulum have connected, ask your questions. If you don't get a clear response, I recommend sleeping with your pendulum under your pillow for at least a week to attune it properly to you.

Runes

Runes are an alphabet or writing system used by the Germanic peoples of Europe, which Norse legends claim were created by Odin. They're also associated with the Norns (the three Norse 'Fates' of the past, present and future).

Runic symbols can be found mostly in Northern Europe at many sacred sites on large stone monuments. They were – and are still – also carved onto jewellery, and they adorned Viking boats and weapons. Runes carved onto 'stones' were also used for divination.

These 'rune stones' are most commonly made out of stone, bones, crystals or wood. Use them either by choosing one intuitively or by throwing several of them onto a surface and then interpreting the results. You can read the symbols that fall face up and likewise interpret the reverse meaning of any that fall upside down. The set I use includes the meanings for both options on the interpretation card for each rune.

To use: after cleansing your runes, attune them to you by sitting with them and allowing your energy to fuse with them. Then you might like to pick just one for general guidance as I do.

Alternatively, you might want to use one of the spreads described on the sheet or book that comes with your runes. This sheet or book will usually explain what each rune means or you can research the topic online.

Please note that runes are an extremely complex system with many, many strands to their history and use. I've provided the briefest of descriptions here to stay focused on the topic for this chapter (divination). I encourage you to research further if it interests you.

Chapter 6: Divination

The Tarot

The Tarot originated as a set of playing cards that later became a divinatory tool. Tarot cards can guide you and help you move through a particular situation, or bring you spiritual messages and clarity on where you need to focus your attention.

Each deck contains two groups of cards called 'Arcana'. The Major Arcana consists of 22 pictured cards that usually herald major changes or turning points in your life. The Minor Arcana cards are very similar to the more familiar playing cards. They contain four suits, each with ten numbered cards (one through ten) and four 'face cards' (the king, queen, knight and page).

Numbered Minor Arcana cards tend to reflect the energy or experiences you're currently going through. Meanwhile, the face cards tend to represent people in your life: people you know, people who've come into your life or even aspects of yourself.

To use: again, cleanse your cards, then draw one card daily for general guidance or try out different spreads for particular questions and clarity on a situation. As with the rune stones above, in most decks (not all), you'll find a book that explains what each card means and provides sample spreads.

However, as I also mentioned above, I encourage you to always go with your intuition first. Only then, if you feel you need to, consult the book that comes with your cards.

Oracle cards

You can use oracle cards for guidance, clarity, peace of mind or inspiration.

Although you can get really intricate answers to your questions, they're often simpler to use than Tarot cards as they're less structured. They also usually have words or meanings printed right on the card, so you can get instant insight into your question.

This means that if you've never read cards before, they're a great place to start.

To use: as with Tarot cards, cleanse your deck, and then either draw a single oracle card or do a spread. Picking a single card each day is an excellent way to connect with your cards and strengthen your intuition.

Scrying

Scrying is the art of looking within the surface of an object to see visions or messages. It's another form of divination that's been around for thousands of years. During that time, it's been used to foretell prophecies, divine futures, gain clarity and guidance, and receive revelations or inspiration.

You can use many different objects to scry, such as:

- a crystal ball
- a black mirror
- any still water
- smoke
- wax dripped onto water
- any reflective surface
- fire
- stones (crystals)
- a black bowl filled with water
- any black glass (eg. obsidian).

You can even just close your eyes and use your closed eyelids as your 'surface' – this is called 'eyelid scrying'.

To use: to successfully scry, you must trust your intuition and not discount anything you see, sense or feel – even if it seems silly or insignificant. You can look for general information or ask specific questions. You can scry your current situation, get answers to questions or possibly even divine future events.

Chapter 6: Divination

Crystal ball scrying

A crystal ball is a powerful magickal tool that you can use for divination.

Crystals balls come in many sizes and can be made of any crystal or clear glass. Clear quartz is best, but I've also seen them made of sodalite, amethyst, rose quartz, obsidian and many more types of stone.

To use: I'd encourage you to start with a true crystal ball (not a clear glass one) while you're learning to get more accurate readings.

You read a true crystal ball by noticing the natural patterns contained within the crystal. With a clear glass ball, on the other hand, you'll read it based on the pictures that first appear as mist within the ball.

Other methods of divination

Reading tea leaves

Truly, reading tea leaves may challenge your divination skills like never before! What you're looking for in the leaves are symbols, letters, pictures or numbers that will tell you a story.

To use: after you finish drinking your tea, turn the cup upside down on a saucer and rotate it anti-clockwise three times. Then turn it back over and rotate it in all directions so that you see as much of the inner surface as possible. Finally, take notes on what you observe, and look up the meanings of anything you see in a book or online.

Reading clouds

Do you take the time to watch the clouds go by? I do and, over the years, I've seen some amazing pictures, including a full, clear Goddess face!

The cloud images you see can have different meanings. For example, they could serve as omens for something, or be signs of good fortune or peace for the world. They may also have a personal meaning that's just for you, which is especially lovely if you've been searching for a sign or an answer.

To use: simply gaze up at the sky and become aware of any pictures or symbols you see, then try to interpret them.

When I saw the Goddess face, I was away from home and on the edge of burnout. I took it as comfort and a message that she was watching over me. As always, if you see something you don't understand, look up its meaning in a book or online.

Reading omens

We've talked about what omens *are* earlier in the chapter – now let's talk about how to work with them.

Have you ever planned something, then had what seemed like a string of unlucky occurrences that seemed to block your way or portend something negative? Or, on the other hand, maybe you'd planned something and all the signs pointed to a good outcome – like waking up to a sunny day when you had an outdoor event.

Either way, you could interpret what happened as an omen.

As with all things, omens only have power when you believe in them. If you do, they could be strong signs from your intuition to protect you from danger or a potentially negative outcome. Or, alternatively, they could confirm that you're on the right path and that your timing is divine.

To use: first, open your awareness. Notice any unusual or repeating occurrences. If you don't understand a sign, look up its meaning in a book or online.

For example, I take a lot of notice of animals. Recently, I had several snake encounters over the course of a few days. I know snakes symbolise transmutation (because they shed their skin), and I just happened to be running a two-day workshop about exactly that. Because of this, I knew the sightings were a fortunate omen!

Chapter 6: Divination

Reading palms

Also known as chiromancy or palmistry, palm reading is the art of foretelling the future through studying the palm. Palm reading can both identify a person's character and foretell their future.

The palmist studies lines, bumps, skin patterns and texture, as well as the general shape of someone's hand. Some readers also include fingers, fingernails and fingerprints in their readings. The size, qualities and intersections of these characteristics all have meanings and messages.

It's a great idea to visit a palmist and have your palms read so you can experience this form of divination for yourself. And, if you're intrigued and want to learn more, there are many online pictorials and books that can teach you how to get started with this fine art.

Ways to use divination in your daily life and magick

- **Consult your pendulum** when you have a direct question that you need an immediate answer to.
- **Do a full oracle or Tarot reading for yourself once a month or even once a year.** Personally, I do mine once a year or whenever I need to. This will help you to walk forward with clarity and direction.
- **Draw an oracle card or a rune stone daily.** This is ideal for general guidance. You could also use oracle or Tarot cards to add more of a particular energy to a spell. For example, I use my Goddess Aphrodite card in love spells.
- **Give yourself a mini tea-leaf reading every time you have a cuppa.**
- **Make yourself a set of decision stones and use it for quick guidance and yes/no answers.** For example, you could use a

white stone to mean 'yes', a black stone to mean 'no', and a neutral stone (or one of a different colour) as the adjudicator. Ask your question clearly, then throw the three stones together. Whichever of the black and white stones is closer to the coloured stone is your answer.

- **Scry whenever you need an answer or a sign for a particular situation.** Look for images and symbols in whatever you're using to scry.
- **Use divination as part of your ritual.** For example, you could be performing a healing spell for someone and do a little card reading that might enlighten them on how to move forward on their healing path.
- **Pay attention.** When you'd like to know if an event is likely to have a good outcome or a negative one, look for omens and signs and pay attention to them.

Your ritual work: a divination ritual

Intention

To get divine guidance, answers to questions or gain clarity.

Timing

Any.

You will need

- Four white candles to mark the directions.
- Representations of each of the elements, and of the Goddess and God for your altar (refer to previous chapters).
- A purple candle.
- A deck of oracle or Tarot cards.
- A picture or representation of Sophia – the goddess of wisdom. You can simply print an image off the internet.

Chapter 6: Divination

- An amethyst crystal.
- Third eye chakra oil (optional). You can find this online (I use a company called Spiritual Sky) or at some discount stores.
- A smudge stick or palo santo stick.
- A lighter.

Ritual steps

1. Find a private space where you won't be disturbed.
2. Gather the tools you'll need and place them on or around your altar. Place the purple candle, the amethyst crystal and the image of Sophia *on* your altar.
3. Cleanse yourself, your circle and all the items you'll use for your ritual with your smudge stick or palo santo stick.
4. Cast the simple circle as you did in Chapter 2.
5. Light the purple candle.
6. Anoint your third eye with the oil (optional).
7. Pass the amethyst crystal through each of the representations of the four elements to consecrate it.
8. Now consecrate the deck of cards with the four elements. Sprinkle it with the salt, pass it through the incense smoke, pass it over the candle flame and sprinkle a few drops of water over it.
9. Holding the cards, close your eyes, take a few deep breaths and ask the goddess Sophia to help you to connect with your inner wisdom.
10. Shuffle the cards, and either ask a specific question or ask for general guidance.
11. Place the deck on the ground or your altar, cut it in half and choose which half you'll read from. Lay the cards out however your intuition tells you to. Use as many as feels right or use an example spread from the book your cards came with.
12. Spend some time pondering the cards. Connect with each of them and trust the answers they give you, even if they're not

the answers you want to hear. Whatever the cards are showing you is for your highest good.

Don't worry if it doesn't make sense right now. It's highly likely that you'll come to understand your reading in the future as events fall into place around you.

13. Close circle in the usual way (see Chapter 2).

How to integrate these teachings into your wholistic lifestyle

- **As I mentioned earlier, the first step to using divination is to listen to your intuition.** Pay attention to ALL the signs, synchronicities, messages in your head and gut feelings. Don't discount anything, and try not to talk yourself out of what you've received, as that will squash down your intuition.

- **If you've never done divination before or you've just dabbled here and there, start slowly.** It can take time to get the hang of what divination feels like and start to get more confident.

- **To begin, I'd suggest getting yourself a set of oracle cards that you're drawn to.** Sleep with them under your pillow for a week or two to attune them to your energies, then begin by drawing one each day and reading its meaning.

- **Once you're feeling confident with those, you might like to try something else like the Tarot or a pendulum.** Your journey with divination is your own; so to have the best experience, you must go with what feels good and right for you.

Chapter 6: Divination

Book of Shadows

☽ Please record your ritual and observations.

☽ You might also like to record information about the different types of divination and divinatory tools and methods.

 Journal tasks

🎩 Please journal any experiences you've had with different divinatory tools, and with using divination for yourself or others.

🎩 Reflect on any times in your life when you received omens or signs that came true and how you felt about it.

Summary – Chapter 6

- Divination is the art of using tools or natural phenomena to connect with both your own intuition and the Divine for insight.
- Most cultures have practised some form of divination for millennia.
- Remember to always cleanse new divination tools and attune them to your energy.
- Divination tools can be very useful in your rituals – for example, you can use a Tarot card to represent a goddess.
- When choosing divination tools, always go with the ones that feel right for you – perhaps because they're visually appealing or functional (eg. crystal cards in crystal healings).

CHAPTER 7

Sacred Spaces

What is sacred space?

A sacred space is a safe, energetically balanced space for you to dwell, work, study, create or do your magick in. Your sacred space can be literally a space within a room, the whole room, a whole house/building or an outdoor space. And you can create it in any way you choose, as long it's pleasing to you and any others who may need to use it.

> A sacred space is a safe, energetically balanced space for you to dwell, work, study, create or do your magick in.

Why create sacred spaces?

Having sacred space within your house can naturally help to maintain more harmony for everyone in it. This is because when you treat a space as sacred, it will usually begin to vibrate at a higher level, which helps with energy flow.

These spaces also help to keep your energy safe and balanced, and can:

- 🧙 help you to focus
- 🧙 inspire your creativity
- 🧙 help to keep your mind clear of clutter
- 🧙 allow the energy around you to flow harmoniously

- help to keep your relationships peaceful
- provide a place to work your rituals that's safe from negative entities or energies.

And there are a million other reasons.

A harmonious home is your everyday sacred space

For some people, home is just a place to store things and rest their heads...

But for the rest of us, our homes are our sanctuaries. Home is a place to rest, rejuvenate and recharge. It's a place to feel safe and connect with our families. A place to find peace and quiet. A place to nourish ourselves.

Every home on Earth is different, and every home has a different dynamic. Whatever your personal situation, though, making your home or a private space within it (like your bedroom) feel more harmonious can be fairly simple.

I work on keeping my whole home as harmonious as possible. However, I also identify specific places within my home as sacred. These include my bedroom and my studio/office. For me, *these are sacred spaces.*

NOTE: You're not limited to just keeping your home harmonious. You can also create harmony and sacred spaces within your business, workplace, garden and more. In this chapter, we'll discuss all of these options. You'll learn how to bring more harmony (and a little magick) to the spaces around you to make them sacred.

Chapter 7: Sacred Spaces

Creating harmony

To start, I'd love to share a few quick and simple tips that you can use right away to bring harmony to your home and/or space:

- **Cleanse your house/space energetically at least once a week.** Or cleanse whenever you feel it needs it – after an argument is especially good.
- **Use sound to shift the energy in a space if it feels slow or heavy.** Use a singing bowl or bell in each room to raise the vibration there.
- **Try energetic cleansing if you feel a little out of sorts before bed, or even a bit unsafe.** Once you're in bed, drift into a semi-meditative state. Then imagine surrounding your whole house with a bubble of white light (as you did in Chapter 2), and demand that any negative entities or energies leave immediately.
- **Perform a cleansing ritual to bring peace back into your realm.** This is especially useful if there's been any tension or disharmony in your home. You could use the visualisation ritual above as an example.
- **Place a black crystal above your front door to repel yucky people.** Set the intention that if someone with negative energy or ill intentions passes your threshold, they'll quickly feel uncomfortable and want to leave.
- **If you live with others, set clear boundaries for yourself.** This one is really important to maintain harmony and lower the likelihood of disagreements and conflict with housemates.

    For example, my husband and I bought a house with my mum and dad. In that dual-living situation, we all had to be very clear about the boundaries that were important to us. Personally, I had to let everyone know about my intense need for privacy and quiet time after I hold any large events to help me recharge and rebalance.

- **Maintain clear lines of communication.** Tell people about your own needs and desires, and try to respect those of the people you live with.

And when things break down (which they sometimes will), talk about what happened as constructively as possible, then clear it energetically. This will not just clear the air but also help you to identify how to avoid the same thing happening again in future.

- **Declutter regularly.** Try to keep your home/space as clear of clutter as you can to allow the energy to flow clearly.

Case study: sacred spaces in action

When I'm working on a project and need to focus, it's important to feel calm, balanced and creatively inspired. This means I need a quiet, private, comfortable space to work in. However, this space can change completely day-to-day according to how I feel.

Today I felt the need to be in Nature. So I lugged all my work supplies up to my lovely pool area, set out a tablecloth and arranged everything how I needed it to be. I made sure I had plenty of water and snacks. Then I energetically prepared myself by smudging, tuning in and balancing my third eye and crown chakras.

Once I'd created my sacred space, I felt far more ready to work.

As I mentioned previously, you can make your whole home a sacred space or you can create many separate, dedicated sacred spaces within it. Here are just a few ideas:

- bedrooms
- business and workplace spaces
- car spaces
- children's spaces
- exercise spaces

> You can make your whole home a sacred space or you can create many separate, dedicated sacred spaces within it.

Chapter 7: Sacred Spaces

- gardens
- kitchens
- self-care spaces
- study spaces.

In the section below, you'll learn *how* to set up sacred space in each of these dedicated areas.

How to make dedicated spaces sacred

Bedroom

You can make your bedroom into whatever kind of sacred space you like. It might be your magickal sacred space, a love nest or your sanctuary of solitude.

Include items around your room that please your eye, such as photos, books, candles, cushions, art, etc. Also consider the colours you use: a red wall or red decorations can inspire passion, while a blue or green room can be calming and peaceful.

Refer to Appendix B for the magickal associations of colours.

Kitchen

I love cooking and a bit of kitchen witchery. When I'm doing a big cook-up – either for weekly food prep or a special event – I like to make my kitchen a sacred space within which to work.

I have a permanent altar set up in there. On it are representations of the four elements (Earth, Air, Fire and Water) and my favourite witch statue. I also include a fresh seasonal representation, such as flowers from my garden.

Then, before I start cooking, I make sure the space is clean and tidy. I'll smudge the area, light a candle on my altar, say a little invocation and then simply let the creative juices flow.

Spaces for children

To provide a safe sanctuary for your children and help them sleep restfully, create sacred space in their bedrooms. You can do this by including items that please them and inspire feelings of happiness, safety and contentment.

You can also redecorate your child's bedroom as they transition through 'coming of age' periods. I remember when I was changing from being a toddler to becoming a young girl, my parents redid my bedroom to mark the transition. They painted my walls in a soft blue, put in white furniture, and gave me a doona cover, curtains and a beanbag made from pretty material with blue and purple clouds on it. I loved to spend hours in that room, just playing contently.

> As with decorating your own bedroom, consider the colours you use and how your children's space fits their functional needs.

As with decorating your own bedroom, consider the colours you use and how your children's space fits their functional needs. For example, is it just a sleep space? Or is it a study space too? Maybe it's also a chill-out or play space?

If your kids have a shared play area, you can make that room a sacred space too. There, the energy that you wish to inspire for them may change each day. For example:

- **To inspire nice, calm 'quiet time'**: smudge first to cleanse the area and balance the energies. Then play some soft meditation music and maybe burn a calming essential oil like lavender.

- **To inspire energetic fun like dancing, jumping around or exercising**: use a singing bowl or bell to raise the vibration, then put on some lively music or get out musical instruments. Finally, anoint each child's sacral chakra with a diluted chakra essential oil blend (if that's safe for them) and burn an uplifting incense or an essential oil like orange.

Chapter 7: Sacred Spaces

🧙 **To inspire creativity:** smudge the space and put on some stirring music like tribal drumming. Then anoint each child's sacral and solar plexus chakras with a diluted essential oil blend (again, if that's safe for them). Lastly, call on the goddess Brigid to light the flame of inspiration atop each of their heads.

Study spaces

Some people love to study, while others find it a real chore. In either case, why not make your study space a sacred one that you enjoy working in? It may just make the process easier or less boring. It also may get your creative juices flowing or help you to focus.

> Some people love to study, while others find it a real chore. In either case, why not make your study space a sacred one that you enjoy working in?

This can apply to study spaces for the whole family or to individual study spaces. You could even take a little 'sacred space creation' travel kit with you if you need to study in a public space like a library (more on travel kits in Chapter 8).

The obvious first step when doing this is to make sure you have everything you need with you, so you don't have to keep getting up and disrupting your study. Basic items would include your study materials, stationery and lots of water and snacks.

Next, add your personal touches to make the space feel nice to hang out in. I like to have flowers, a candle and incense burning, my chakra oils and maybe a crystal or two. Also consider where your study desk/table is placed. I prefer to be near a window as I have a penchant for looking outside when I'm thinking: it just helps to clear my head.

Finally, before you start to work or study, cleanse your space first. I sometimes use my singing bowl to raise the vibration if I feel the space needs it, and I cleanse my computer, phone and books.

> **Handy tip for study spaces**
> Rainbow fluorite is an excellent crystal for study. It helps with mental focus and clarity, as well as helping you to retain information.

Garden spaces

Whether you're a mad-keen gardener or not, having a sacred space in your garden is lovely not only for you but also for any magickal beings and animals. You might like to have well-planned garden beds, a full-on permaculture garden, or just a nice spot to sit and hang out in. Whatever you'd like your sacred garden space to be, consider the following:

- **What do you want your garden to do?** Will it feed you, give you privacy, be a space to relax in or be a space for ritual?
- **Will you need some furniture?** Perhaps you'd like a seat or a little altar table?
- **Considering the above, plan your sacred garden space layout.** My garden was fully landscaped when we moved in, so I claimed just a little rectangle of space and dubbed it my 'Witch Garden'.
- **Keep the space tidy as best you can.** Garden clutter still counts as clutter!
- **If you have weeds, are they useful?** If you're not sure, research the magickal and medicinal properties of herbs that are commonly seen as weeds.
- **Consider the animals and magickal beings you'd like to attract into your garden.** For example, you could:
  - Put out some sort of water bowl or vessel for animals and insects, or hang a bird feeder in one of your trees.
  - If you want to attract more of a certain animal energy, consider the plants that most appeal to that animal. For

Chapter 7: Sacred Spaces

example, bees are associated with prosperity, so if you want to create more prosperity, you could plant more bee-attracting herbs and flowers. (See Appendix F for more animal associations.)

- Regularly leave offerings for the guardians of North, South, East and West, or for specific magickal beings you'd like to work with.
- Consider planting herbs or flowers that are associated with any magickal beings you'd like to work with. For example, if you wanted to work with faeries, you might consider researching and planting the flowers they most like.

Business spaces

Making your business space sacred can help to attract more customers and more prosperity. It can also help to keep energies flowing for productive work and positive vibes for a happy workspace.

> No matter what type of business you run, you can keep your space sacred and the vibes high.

No matter what type of business you run, you can keep your space sacred and the vibes high. Here are a few specific suggestions:

- **Cleanse the space regularly with a sage stick, sage spray or palo santo stick.** Personally, I cleanse my salon after every client, but even once a week would be beneficial.
- **Consider the décor, colours and branding of your business.** Do they please you? Do they align with what you're selling? Do they emit the energy you want? My business is magickal, so my colours are purple and black, which go hand in hand in my mind!
- **Keep live flowers or plants around.** These emit good energies and help to make the space more harmonious.
- **Place crystals around you to create the energies you want, eg. prosperity and positivity.** You can also use them to

cleanse your computer or put them in your cash till to attract more sales. See Appendix C for more information about which crystals do what.

- 🧙 **Place black crystals (eg. obsidian or black tourmaline) or herbs around the main entrance of your business.** As with putting a black crystal over the door of your home, this will repel yucky people and negative energies.

Workplace spaces

If you work for someone else, this can be trickier – but it can still be done. You may just need to be more subtle about it.

For example, when I used to work in a corporate office, I covered my desk in photos, crystals, wall art and a Buddha statue. I'd regularly surround my desk with a ring of salt too, and I did a weekly crystal spell to absorb and deflect negative energies. I know I was lucky: my bosses let me get away with a lot because I worked really hard and my desk was out of sight of any customers.

However, you don't need to be as obvious about it as I was. You could use simpler techniques like:

- 🧙 energetically cleansing your workspace with the 'bubble of white light' technique (see Chapter 2 for this)
- 🧙 using a sage spray – maybe weekly or whenever you feel the space needs it
- 🧙 putting a few carefully chosen crystals on your desk
- 🧙 carrying crystals on you to create the energy you want around you.

Be aware that all of these techniques can have a ripple effect. You may end up making your customers and workmates more positive and happy too!

> *Be aware that all of these techniques can have a ripple effect. You may end up making your customers and workmates more positive and happy too!*

Chapter 7: Sacred Spaces

That said, you should be able to gauge for yourself how obvious you can be about creating a sacred workspace. Feel into your boss's and colleagues' comfort levels. Try to be respectful, while doing what you need to be a calm, happy and productive employee.

Self-care spaces

You can make any self-care activity more sacred and magickal by making the space in which you perform it sacred. Think about the self-care rituals you already practise – perhaps having a bath, giving yourself a pedicure, washing your hair or any activity that's about caring for you. You could very simply make any of these more sacred by:

- casting a gentle circle of white light around your space to keep the energies positive
- cleansing the space with sage, sandalwood or frankincense
- lighting candles
- placing some fresh greenery or flowers around you
- including some specially chosen crystals
- invoking the goddess Aphrodite or Venus
- burning some nurturing essential oils in an oil burner.

Exercise spaces

It might seem a little weird to think of creating a sacred exercise space but, seriously, it can help to motivate, energise and focus you! If you go to the gym, take some really uplifting energy music with you (personally, I crank up the heavy metal). Or, if you exercise at home, cleanse the space first. Then:

> It might seem a little weird to think of creating a sacred exercise space but, seriously, it can help to motivate, energise and focus you!

- burn some uplifting essential oils
- use your singing bowl or bell to raise the vibration in the room
- play some energetic tunes.

If you struggle with exercise, get outside for a natural energy lift. Remember: Nature herself is a sacred space!

Car spaces

If you like to travel with a bit of extra protection and comfort, making your car space sacred is simple. If I'm driving on a long-distance trip, I like to surround my car with a big bubble of white light while I invoke my guides and ask them to keep us safe from harm, breakdown and danger.

I also have a little mini-diffuser that hangs off my mirror and emits essential oils to keep my car smelling magickal, while also keeping me alert. You might like to keep crystals for clarity, focus, safety and protection in the console as well.

Spaces away from home

I'll just touch on this briefly here, as I'll go into much more detail about travel magick in Chapter 8. For now, I'll simply say that if you're going on holiday, travelling for work or need to stay away from home, you can make wherever you're staying sacred. This can help you to feel more 'at home' and comfortable while you're away.

Create a travel pack with some crystals, oracle cards, your sage smudge spray, and perhaps a tealight candle if it's safe to include one. Also take your journal and a pen, and whatever else you need to maintain your inner harmony and sense of safety.

Preparing your sacred space

When you set up a sacred space, the first step in preparing it is clearing it of any clutter to create a clear energy flow. Then give it a good clean and vacuum or dust it if needed.

Next, give the whole room a good cleansing smudge. If you have a besom (magickal broom), you can also use it at this point to sweep any negative energies right out the door.

Chapter 7: Sacred Spaces

After this, consider where you want to place any furniture for good flow. Think about the colours you could use to enhance the energies you want. Then ask yourself which items you'll need – for example, books, candles or crystals.

Finally, have fun setting it all up until it feels just right. Optionally, you might also like to say a blessing over your sacred space to consecrate it.

Ideally, you'll then cleanse your space again each time you use it.

Tools to create a sacred space

You don't need to spend a great deal of money to create a sacred space. Instead, you can easily use whatever you already have around your house. That said, a few tools that would be handy to have on hand to set up and maintain clear, positive energies in any space are:

- a smudge stick, sage spray or palo santo stick
- a besom to sweep away negative energies (although any broom will do)
- a good supply of candles in different colours to mark quarters or use in ritual work – tealights are fine
- matches or a lighter.

Your ritual work: harmonious home ritual

Intention

To create a harmonious home.

(Note that you can adapt this ritual however you please to suit you, your family or your housemates.)

Timing

Ideally during a New or Waxing Moon, but really, any time is good for this sort of work.

You will need

- A smudge stick.
- Photos or tokens of everyone who lives within your home. A token can be anything personal, like a photo, a piece of jewellery or a crystal they love.
- A rose quartz crystal.
- Fresh flowers with the stalks removed, so you just have the heads.
- A large (salad bowl-sized) bowl of water.
- A white candle for each person who lives within the house – tealights would be ideal.
- A jar with a label you've made yourself that says 'Harmony Jar'.
- Small (at least 5cm) pieces of pink paper, cut up into any shapes you like.
- A pink pen.

Ritual steps

1. Begin by preparing your sacred space. It may be a good idea to do this ritual in the room where everyone congregates together the most.
2. Arrange all the tools you'll need for the ritual on your altar, on a table or even on the floor.
3. If at all possible, gather everyone who lives within the house to take part in the ritual.
4. Smudge the space and invite everyone present to smudge also.
5. Call on Hestia – the Greek goddess of the hearth and home – to witness and bless your ritual.
6. Light the central white candle and then cast a basic circle as you did in Chapter 2.

Chapter 7: Sacred Spaces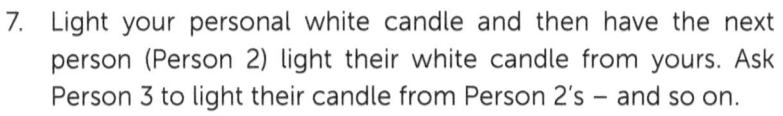

7. Light your personal white candle and then have the next person (Person 2) light their white candle from yours. Ask Person 3 to light their candle from Person 2's – and so on.

   Alternatively, if you're performing this ritual alone, you can light each candle from the previous one yourself. Ensure you think of the person that each candle represents as you light it.

8. Now give everyone a piece of the pink paper, and – going around in a circle – ask everyone to write something positive (in the pink pen) that they'd like to bring into the house.

   Or, if they'd prefer, they can write something positive about another member of the household. Everyone can have as many turns writing things on the pieces of paper as they'd like.

   If you're doing the ritual alone, you can simply write something to represent each person.

   Regardless, place all of the pieces of paper in the 'Harmony Jar' one by one.

9. When everyone is done, give each person a flower and have them place it in the bowl of water. Alternatively, place one flower for each person into the bowl yourself. As you do, say:

   "As one, we invite peace, harmony
   and more love into our home.
   We also bring compassion and
   kindness beneath this dome.
   We honour each other's personal space, and if
   challenges arise, we speak with respect to their face.
   And to each of you now I say unto thee,
   by the will of us all, so mote it be!"

10. Thank each person present for attending and making the commitment to bring more harmony to your household. It might be nice to hug each other at this point if that feels comfortable.

11. Thank the goddess Hestia for attending your ritual, and close your circle in the usual way.

12. If it's safe to, leave the white candles burning until they burn out. Also leave the flowers, photos and rose quartz crystal in place for as long as you can.

    Either leave the 'Harmony Jar' there too or put it in a prominent place in your home where everyone can see it. Also place more pieces of pink paper and the pink pen near it in case people would like to add more positive notes at any time.

How to integrate these teachings into your wholistic lifestyle

- **If it isn't already, make your house into a home.** Make it comfortable by placing things around it that please you to look at. Make it cosy and make it *yours*.
- **Try to be aware at all times of how the energy in your house feels.** Does it feel heavy or light? Is it flowing or are there any spots that feel really stagnant?
- **Give your house a good spring clean.** Remember that decluttering also moves stagnant energy.
- **Cleanse your house regularly to keep the energy flowing.** If you're using a smudge stick, it's a good idea to give your house a good vacuum afterwards to fully remove the negative energy.
- **Keep harmonising crystals around your house to keep the energy feeling good.** Rose quartz will emit the energy of love, while blue lace agate will give the energy of clear communication.
- **Burn chakra candles or oils around your home** (after checking that everyone is happy with the scent). This will keep everyone's chakras nice and harmonised.
- **Perform the above ritual whenever it starts to feel necessary.** This can help to maintain harmony between everyone in the house.

Chapter 7: Sacred Spaces

🧙 **Create various sacred spaces around your home.** To really benefit everyone, involve each member of the house who will use that space.

Book of Shadows

☽ Please record your ritual and observations.

☽ Record the information about different types of sacred spaces for reference.

🪶 Journal tasks

🧙 Make notes on how you can bring more harmony to your home right now, and then pick a space that you'd like to make sacred. What items do you have around the house that you could use right away to change the energy?

🧙 For a full list of associations to help you in setting up your sacred space, eg. colour meanings, crystal meanings, herbs and incenses, please refer to the Appendices.

Summary - Chapter 7

- 🧹 A sacred space is one that's safe and energetically balanced for you to dwell, work, study, create or do your magick in.
- 🧹 You can set up sacred everyday spaces that are dedicated to specific activities like cooking, studying, exercising and working.
- 🧹 Creating sacred spaces is a skill that's important for everyday life: sacred spaces help to keep your mind clear, help you to focus and nurture your creativity.
- 🧹 A peaceful, harmonious home is a kind of everyday sacred space that helps to keep the energy within it (and the energy of its inhabitants) balanced.
- 🧹 Creating a sacred space is essential for ritual and spellwork because the best magickal results require clear, flowing energy.

CHAPTER 8

Keeping Your Magick with You

You can practise magick anywhere, anytime

So far, you've probably completed most of the magickal tasks in this book inside at home or outside in your garden. But what happens when you walk out the front door? Do you need to take all your supplies and tools with you?

Just in case you don't already know by now, I'm here to tell you that **you ARE your magick**. You don't need a load of tools or supplies with you to perform spells or live magickally. I've successfully used nothing more than simple, focused intention and energy to work magick many times.

> You ARE your magick.

Having said that, I do enjoy using certain tools, both to help me focus and for guidance when I'm away. And I use them whether I'm heading out of town or just down the road.

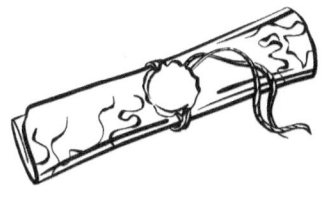

> ### Here's what I like to carry with me when I leave my house...
>
> I often carry crystals and magick sprays around with me for general use. I also just can't help but take a deck of oracle or Tarot cards with me when I meet a friend for coffee or lunch!
>
> Beyond that, I always take a mini 'magick kit' – which usually consists of my sprays, chakra oils and a grounding essential oil blend – to expos and markets.
>
> And finally, I always, ALWAYS take a magickal travel kit with me when I go away.

Creating a 'mobile magick' kit

Even if you can't leave any magickal items at all lying around or take them with you, you can perform mini-rituals 'on the go'. Options include using incantations, focused intention, meditation, chanting or even invisible sigils you draw onto your skin.

But if you *can* bring one or two items with you, think hard about what to take. Anything you choose to place on a mini-altar or in a travel kit needs to easily fit into your bag to carry with you. This means it needs to be small – think of items like:

- Crystals.
- Essential oils and magickal sprays (eg. a sage smudge spray).
- Items from Nature like feathers, leaves or stones.
    Note: always collect these items respectfully; and if you're travelling overseas, check first whether you're allowed to bring them into the country. Some countries have very strict biosecurity restrictions – at best, border security officers may

Chapter 8: Keeping Your Magick with You

take your items away. At worst, you may face a fine of up to many thousands of dollars.

- A palo santo stick for cleansing – it's smaller and easier to transport than a smudge stick.
- That said, again, if you're travelling overseas, double-check whether you're allowed to bring this wood into the country.
- Talismans (eg. a 'safe-travel talisman') that you can wear on your wrist so it doesn't take up room.
- Tealight candles and a lighter or matches.
- Note: if you're flying, please check with your airline first about taking a lighter on the plane.
- Meditations downloaded onto your phone.
- A journal and magickal books to read.
- A deck of Tarot or oracle cards.

Other places you might want to cast your magick

Following are a few of the places away from home where you might find yourself wanting to work magick. I've included options that involve both tool-free magick and using small, portable tools.

When you travel

As I mentioned previously, I always take a mobile magickal travel kit when I go away. Whether I'm only going a few hours away for a short trip or overseas, I like to have certain special items on hand – just in case I need them.

I *always* make protection talismans, both for myself and any family members who are

> Whether I'm only going a few hours away for a short trip or overseas, I like to have certain special items on hand – just in case I need them.

travelling too, which we wear the whole time we're away. Additionally, I usually take:

- at least one protection crystal
- my favourite deck of oracle cards
- something to cleanse with (a smudge stick or palo santo stick)
- maybe a tealight candle or two
- something magickal to read
- my journal.

However, the exact items in my travel kit change every time I travel, depending on how I'm feeling, where I'm going and why I'm travelling. In the same way, your travel kit should contain whatever feels right and good to you.

At work or school

This one's a bit trickier because you're in a space where there are other people – but there are still things you can do.

I talked quite a bit in the last chapter about all the magickal things I used to keep on my desk at my corporate job. However, I also know that not everyone is as blessed with an understanding boss and workmates as I was.

If your workplace or classroom isn't quite so liberal, here are a few things you could try:

- Surround yourself with a bubble of white light every day before you leave for your workplace or school.
- Give yourself a mini energy healing session using chakra exercises or tapping during your break if you're feeling stressed or under the pump.
- Keep a black tourmaline or obsidian crystal on you, in your desk drawer or on your desk to absorb negative energies. Cleanse it once a week under running water.
- Keep different crystals for different purposes in your bra or desk drawer. For example, try rose quartz for love or

Chapter 8: Keeping Your Magick with You

bloodstone for prosperity. You can find more crystal correspondences in Appendix C. Again, be sure to cleanse your crystals once a week.

- Use cleansing essential oils such as frankincense or sandalwood on yourself. Remember to always dilute them with a carrier oil like coconut or grapeseed first.
- Try composing an on-the-spot chant to clear your head or find an answer if you're feeling stuck on something. You can use any words you like, as long as they focus on the issue.
- Keep a container of salt at your desk, and really sneakily place a fine ring of it around your workspace once a week.
- Rather than scoping out social media during your break, what about reading a magickal book?

When you go out 'on the town'

- First, surround yourself with a protective bubble of white light before you leave the house. If you're drinking beforehand, do this before you start.
- Then consider taking a protective crystal with you and wearing it when you head out. Ideas might include black tourmaline, onyx, obsidian or tiger's eye – you can find other options in Appendix C.
- Wherever you go, please trust your intuition. If something doesn't feel right, just don't go there! Your intuition is trying to keep you safe, so trust it.

For your business

The best thing about owning your own business is that you can do whatever you like – yay! So in my studio, I have the works! That means:

- a bowl of crystals
- essential oils
- incense
- magickal sprays

- oracle cards
- protective talismans
- smudging tools
- talismans for prosperity and attraction
- a jade plant for prosperity outside my door.

> Creating a sacred business space is ALL about the intention.

The key is to include items in your business space that resonate with you – ideally, ones that will bring more business through the door and ultimately help your clients. And yes, if your business is online, you can apply the same principles. Creating a sacred business space is ALL about the intention.

Additionally, if you're going to a business event, you can blend a 'success oil' – perhaps to keep you calm, imbue you with confidence and/or make a good impression. Check out the herbs in Appendix G for ideas about oils you could include in this blend. You could also do some calming or energising energy work before you go – or perhaps even once you get there.

Case study: magick at a big business event

I was holding my first stall at a big event after rebranding as 'Wiccid' and I was feeling a bit stressed and out of sorts, which was *not* conducive to meeting lots of potential clients and enjoying a successful night!

So just before the event, I took myself away into a corner and did some quick energy work. First, I cleansed myself, then I tuned in to my centre to bring balance and calm. And what followed was an AH-mazing night! My table was buzzing with people all night, and I was on fire!

I have no doubt that this simple exercise contributed to a successful night.

Chapter 8: Keeping Your Magick with You

When you're playing sports

Whether you play a team sport or some kind of individual activity, you can use magick to help keep you safe and enhance your personal performance. Now I'm not talking about changing the result of a game – that involves messing with others! Instead, I'm recommending you use magick to help you do your best, which may be for the good of all.

To keep you safe, surround yourself with a bubble of white light before the game or training. You can also use essential oils or protective crystals. Again, see Appendix C for crystals – but be careful about wearing these if you play a contact sport!

> To help you perform at your personal peak, you obviously have to do the necessary training, but you could enhance this with a success spell.

To help you perform at your personal peak, you obviously have to do the necessary training, but you could enhance this with a success spell. And if your team would be on board with the idea, you could also write a magickal chant to all perform together before each game.

Your ritual work: safe travel

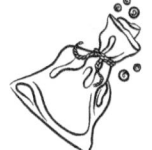

Intention

To keep you, plus any companions with you and your belongings, safe when you're travelling – whether to another town, state or overseas.

Timing

Any, but during the New or Waxing Moon is always ideal if possible.

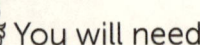

You will need

- A smudge stick.
- All altar representations (see Chapter 2), including the white candle.
- A red candle.
- A red pen.
- A hand-drawn map that includes your current location and where you're going.
- Embroidery thread in blue (sky), green (water) and yellow (land) – use whatever colour shades please you, as long as each colour represents one of those three things to you.
- Scissors.
- One red jasper crystal for each suitcase you'll be taking.
- Some fresh or dried basil. (If the basil is dried, ideally use something organic that you've dried yourself.)

Ritual steps

1. Begin by preparing yourself and your sacred space.
2. Arrange all the tools you'll need on your altar or table, except the crystal/s, herbs, thread and scissors, which can sit on the floor nearby. Place the red candle in the middle and the map in front of it.
3. After everything for your ritual is ready to go, you might like to have a purification bath or shower, perhaps with a salt scrub as per previous rituals.
4. Smudge yourself, the space and all your tools/supplies.
5. Light the central white altar candle, and then cast a basic circle as you learnt in Chapter 2.
6. Light your red candle, then use your red pen to write an 'X' on your current location on the map and another 'X' on your destination. Draw a dotted line between the two 'X's.
7. Decide where you'd like to wear the safe-travel talisman cord you're going to make (I usually put mine on my wrist). Then

Chapter 8: Keeping Your Magick with You

take your embroidery threads, measure out 1.5 times the diameter of that body part for each colour, and plait them together into a simple cord.

As you plait, chant:

> *"By Earth, by Air, by Sea*
> *Safe during my travels I shall be.*
> *By Earth, by Air, by Sea*
> *Goddess watches over and protects me.*
> *By Earth, by Air, by Sea*
> *Until safely home again I be*
> *By Earth, by Air, by Sea*
> *Safe and protected I shall be."*

As with all of the chants in this book, please feel free to change the wording to something that resonates better if you need to.

8. If you'd like to make cords for other people, ask them first. If they're happy to wear one, simply insert their name instead of 'I' in the second line of the chant. Then use 'her/him/them' in the fourth line instead of 'me', and 'she/he/they' in the sixth and eighth line instead of 'I'.

   Another nice touch if you're making a cord for another person is to have them hold it while you plait it to imbue it with their energy.

9. Place the cord/s on top of the map.

10. Speak your intention into each jasper crystal in turn, asking it to keep your luggage/belongings safe. Place each one on the map too.

11. Sprinkle the map and other items with the basil, saying:

> *"From the moment I/we leave my/our humble abode,*
> *safe from harm, danger or upset I/we shall be.*
> *During my/our travels on the road,*
> *whether by the air, the sea or the land,*
> *protected I/we be by the Goddess's hand.*
> *By the power of three times three,*
> *until I/we return safe, so shall this be."*

12. Snuff out the candles, then leave everything else as it is at least overnight or for three days if possible.
13. Close circle in the usual way, as you learnt in Chapter 2.
14. Before you close each suitcase, put one of the empowered red jasper crystals inside it among your things.
15. Tie your talisman cord on, knotting it well. Wear it from the moment you leave your home until the moment you return. Don't remove it, even for a shower. If you're going for a longish trip, I suggest adding a little glue to the knot of the talisman to make sure the cord stays on.
16. Once you're home safe, you can remove your talisman, and either bury or burn it.

    Your spell is now done.

How to integrate these teachings into your wholistic lifestyle

- **You could begin making mini-altars around your home for practice.** Just put whatever feels good on them. Refer to Chapter 7 for inspiration.
- **Be mindful of what you need magickally at all times.** For example, other than basic necessities like food and water:
  - Do you feel like you need protection when you go out?
  - Do you need certain crystals to help you focus at work or school?
  - Are there essential oils that could help to keep you healthy (for example, I use one called 'DigestZen' for my tummy)?

  Incorporate these kinds of things as a natural part of your basic daily routine. Use them at home before you leave. Either carry them on you or pack them in your bag.
- **Draw sigils such as protection sigils on your skin with body cream when you hop out of the shower.**

Chapter 8: Keeping Your Magick with You

- Plan out your magickal kit for when you're travelling – see earlier in the chapter for ideas of what to include (and warnings!)
- If you're an empath who picks up on other people's energies, I strongly suggest protecting your own energy at all times, especially out in public. At the very least, create a bubble of white light around yourself before you leave home.
- Carry crystals with you for different purposes like health, energy, protection, prosperity, etc. Trying keeping them in your bra, bag or pocket. This might be one of the easiest ways to protect yourself before you play any sports (again, for non-contact sports only!)
- Perform rituals whenever and wherever you need them. For example, do a full ritual at home before you leave for a trip or a mini-ritual when you're out and about. Experiment with using no tools, and use intent, incantations or chants to raise and direct energy instead.
- If you pack a lunch for work or school, put a little kitchen witchery into your food and then eat the magick when you need it!
- Make yourself up some little oil blends that you can easily carry with you and apply when needed. Find recipes in books or make them up after doing some research. I have a success blend that I've used for years when I'm going to job interviews or business events with glowing results.

Book of Shadows

- ☽ Please record your ritual and observations.
- ☽ You might also like to record the list of small items you can include on mini-altars or in travel kits as a quick reference.

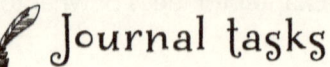

 Journal tasks

🎩 Journal ways in which you could start taking your magick with you.

Summary – Chapter 8

- 🧹 Your magick comes from within you: your tools and supplies are simply an aid to help you focus and amplify energies.
- 🧹 You can work magick using nothing more than intention, visualisation, chanting and energy raising.
- 🧹 You can perform magick anytime and anywhere – when you're travelling, at work, at school, out for a social night or at an event.
- 🧹 If you're away from home, having some of your supplies with you can empower you to create the outcomes you want as well as help you to focus.
- 🧹 I recommend creating a 'mobile magick' kit that you can take with you when you travel or when you're out and about.

CHAPTER 9

Your Circle

Who's in your circle?

Your circle is – to put it simply – the people you surround yourself with. It's your family, friends, associates, classmates, teammates and work colleagues.

It's essential for your wellbeing to surround yourself with positive people who lift you up, inspire you, encourage you and cheer you on when you're kicking arse at life. It's very difficult to keep your energy positive when you have naysayers around who don't support your lifestyle, dreams, goals or successes.

Make a conscious choice about who you spend your time with

Not all of us are naturally blessed with supportive people in our circles. Ask yourself:

- Do you sometimes hang out with someone and then feel tired and drained after your time together?
- Are there people around you who only have negative things to say when you start a new venture or experience success in your life?
- Do some friends constantly whinge and moan about their lives without ever making any moves to improve their situations?

Wholistic Witchcraft

- Do some people around you just not understand your path (for example, this study) and try to talk you out of anything that helps you better your life?
- Do you work with someone who's really not a nice person?

> *Hanging out with people who make you question your worth or make you feel 'less than' lowers your vibration.*

If so, then for your own wellbeing, it might be time to release these people from your life, even if it's just temporary until they can sort themselves out. Hanging out with people who make you question your worth or make you feel 'less than' lowers your vibration. Sometimes, they lower it enough that you start to believe what they say.

Part of the reason these people lower your vibration is that they act like vampires who suck the energy from you to fuel themselves. And if they don't support you in bettering yourself and evolving, they can also prevent you from moving forward, effectively keeping you stuck in the same place.

On the other hand, hanging out with people who believe in you, trust you and love you raises your vibration because it helps you to understand your worth. How? Well...

- People who are there for you when you're feeling low raise your vibration because they help you to heal – sometimes just by being there.
- People who'll lend you an ear and then give you honest, sound advice when you need it will raise your vibration by grounding you and reconnecting you to your integrity.
- People who are doing amazing things in their own lives raise your vibration because they naturally encourage and inspire you to do better.
- People who celebrate your successes with you raise your vibration by making you feel energetically uplifted and supported.

Chapter 9: Your Circle

☽. Case study: the magick of letting go

A few years ago now, I released several people from my life who made me feel heavy, judged, tired and not good enough when I was with them. I'd been friends with them for over ten years, so this was not an easy process – and yes, it hurt.

BUT. Once they were gone, I didn't miss them, which was how I knew I'd made the right decision. My life seemed to instantly improve. I felt lighter. Things felt easier because I wasn't dealing with their daily dramas. I also felt better about myself because I no longer had anyone in my ear telling me that I couldn't do what I wanted in my life.

And the space that opened up when they left made room for new friends – who are AMAZING!

My new friends cheer me on, support me and inspire me with the goals they're crushing in their own lives. They love me for exactly who I am and always make me feel like I'm 'enough'.

Releasing people from your circle

So how do you begin the process of releasing people from your circle? Allow me to share a few tried and tested tips below.

When it's someone in your family

If the negative nelly is a family member, releasing them can be a bit tricky. How can you remove yourself from their bad juju, especially if you live together?

First, I recommend taking an open, honest look at your relationship. Is there somewhere you need to give more nurturing and time that might help to heal it? And do you

> Do you actually *want* to resolve the situation, or are you content to simply remove yourself from it?

actually *want* to resolve the situation, or are you content to simply remove yourself from it?

Depending on your answers, here are a few of the things I do.

If I know I want to resolve the situation, I first prepare:

- If there's been quarrelling, negative emotion or illness in my home, I completely cleanse the house with a smudge stick. I'll often use my singing bowl in every room to lift the vibration too.
- I've also successfully performed harmonious home and love rituals (see Chapter 7).
- I'll sometimes write a letter to the person causing the disharmony, in which I pour out all my feelings. Then I burn the letter to release the negative energy between us. This can help to clear things a bit.
- Next, I take practical steps to rebalance and calm myself. Once I'm back in balance, I can observe the other person's behaviour objectively and understand how I might be reflecting some of it – or even contributing to it – myself. I can then do some healing around it.
- I make sure I have firm boundaries in place around how I'd like to be treated, and around what is and isn't acceptable behaviour.

Then, once I'm ready:

- I'm a talker, so I'll often try to talk constructively to the other person to bring light and healing to the situation.
- If that's too hard, I've also expressed myself in writing with a letter. Sometimes, depending on how I write, this can be a more gentle way of communicating. And it can often be more effective than a conversation if the other person isn't 'hearing' me when I speak to them.
- If the disharmony is happening because someone in my home or circle is feeling genuinely poorly (for example, if

they're stressed, afraid or sick), I do what I can to nurture them.

But if that doesn't work, or if I decide not to resolve it at that time:

- 🧹 I literally physically remove myself from their presence. I might retreat to my room, go out in the yard or hang out in my studio.
- 🧹 Sometimes, I'll go and hang out with my friends because they raise my vibration.
- 🧹 I generally also avoid inviting the person in question to spend time with me. This can give us both space to breathe and think.

Unfortunately, some of us do have members of our family who are just genuinely awful people and are really bad for our wellbeing.

I have one of these, and I've realised that my best course of action with this person is to stay the hell away. I have nothing to do with them whatsoever and that arrangement works great for both of us. There's no guilt or shame: just self-preservation.

> Some of us do have members of our family who are just genuinely awful people and are really bad for our wellbeing.

When it's a work colleague

This one can be tricky too, especially if you have to work closely with someone or you love your job and they're the only thing ruining your experience. I can tell you that I've worked with some truly difficult people (and just plain arseholes). Here are a few things that have worked for me.

- 🧹 **Be polite in your dealings.** You don't have to like someone or even be nice to them: just be cordial at all times and keep your own vibration high.

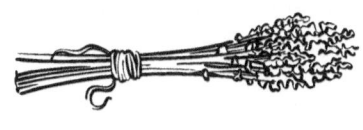

As a bonus, mean people really hate this, because it often reflects their own negative behaviour back at them like a mirror, giving them something to look at.

- **Keep an onyx crystal on your desk/work station.** Point it towards whoever's aiming their bad vibes at you. Before you place the crystal, rinse it in purified water and empower it with words and with your breath.

    For example, you could say to it:

    > *"I charge you to keep all negative energy and people away from me. I only allow positive energy and dealings into my space."*

    Recharge it weekly.

- **Arrive at work before everyone else if you can.** When you get there, place a ring of protective salt around your workspace as you learnt in Chapter 8. Again, do this each week.

- **Energise your throat chakra.** Then try talking to the person in question to see if you can bring more harmony to your workplace. If this doesn't work, you could ask your boss for a mediation session.

- **If a mean co-worker seems to have it in for you, do a freezer spell to 'freeze' their nasty behaviour.** This can be as simple as writing their name on a bit of paper and putting it in an ice cube tray.

- **If you have to sit near the unpleasant workmate, speak to your boss about moving elsewhere.**

- **Or, finally, if you're not particularly attached to your job, start looking for a new one.**

When it's an associate

When I say 'associate' here, I'm talking about people around the outside of your circle: friends of friends, partners of friends or business associates. Sometimes, even if you're not close to people, they may

Chapter 9: Your Circle

feel yucky or make *you* feel yucky when you're around them. And sometimes, you simply don't gel with them.

I've definitely had the experience of not liking a friend's partner. This made it awkward to spend time with my friend because she always wanted to bring her partner. I've experienced the same with friends of friends, and people I see at business functions who can be hard to avoid when we go to the same events. This is how I suggest dealing with those awkward moments:

> Sometimes, even if you're not close to people, they may feel yucky or make *you* feel yucky when you're around them.

- **Energetically protect yourself.** Surround yourself in a protective bubble of white light before you have to go into the energy field of this person.
- **Wear crystals to protect your energy.** These could include black tourmaline, tiger's eye, obsidian, onyx or hematite.
- **As with work colleagues, try to be cordial at all times.** Remember that maintaining the higher ground keeps your vibration high.
- **Try to understand the other person.** Even if you've picked up bad energy or juju from someone, it may help to get to know them and their story even a bit to understand where they're coming from. This sometimes allows you to come from a kinder, more compassionate place.
- **Try doing Ho'opono'pono to clear the negative energy between you.** This is a gentle, almost meditative Hawaiian forgiveness technique that can help you to release any feelings of shame or guilt you're carrying. There are some beautiful YouTube videos that can take you through the process.
- **Talk it out.** On the other hand, if they're genuinely unpleasant, try constructively communicating your feelings and see if you can come to an understanding. If you do this,

however, do your best to come from a loving, tactful place if you want a positive outcome.

- **Talk to your friend.** If the issue is with the partner or friend of a friend, tell your friend how you feel about that person. Make it clear that while you respect their right to make their own choices, you choose not to spend time with that person. Then ask your friend not to bring that person with them to your house/workplace.
- **Finally, if necessary, try to just stay away from the person.** If you're not up to it, do your best to avoid events you know they'll be at.

When it's a teammate

If you play a team sport, and you're finding it hard to play nicely with someone, try one of these tips:

- **Surround yourself with a bubble of protective white light (see Chapter 2).** Do this before every training session or game.
- **Try speaking to the teammate in question.** See if you can find a way to work together.
- **If that fails, try speaking to your captain/coach.** Perhaps they can help to resolve the issue.
- **Wear a protective crystal when you're training/playing.** Again, however, don't do this if you're playing a contact sport!
- **Try casting a freezer spell.** You'll find the details described above in the 'work colleagues' section.
- **If all of this fails, see if you can switch teams.** Sometimes, walking away is the best solution.

When it's a classmate

These tips are suitable for students of all ages – even younger kids with guidance:

Chapter 9: Your Circle

- 🜛 **Surround yourself with a bubble of protective white light.** Do this before you leave the house.
- 🜛 **Wear a protective crystal.** Keep it on you whenever you're in class or at the facility where you're learning.
- 🜛 **Try speaking to the classmate in question.** See if you can find a way to work together.
- 🜛 **If that fails, try speaking to your teacher/professor.** As with speaking to the coach/captain above, see if they can help to resolve your issues.
- 🜛 **Try the freezer spell.** Again, if someone's being mean in a way that will affect your studies, perform the freezer spell described in the 'work colleagues' section.
- 🜛 **If none of the above work, ask if you can move to a different class.** Or, alternatively, try to sit as far away as possible from the person you are having issues with.

And possibly hardest of all: when it's a friend

Along with letting go of family, letting go of a close friend can be one of the hardest things to do. Unlike with other people in your circle, you've actively *chosen* to share a part of yourself with this friend. You've let them in, trusted them, confided in them, possibly introduced them to your family and other friends and allowed them to be a part of your life.

So when they let you down or betray you, or you realise that they're being a negative influence in your life, it really hurts. It can also make you doubt yourself and your ability to judge people's character. You may find yourself wondering, "Why did I trust them in the first place?"

> Releasing friends is up there in trickiness with releasing family.

Releasing friends is up there in trickiness with releasing family, and sometimes your response can vary depending on your specific situation.

For example, if a friend deliberately betrays me, they're gone – bam!

However, if they let me down with no intention of hurting me, I might decide to give them a second chance. Of course, if they THEN let me down again, they're gone too.

Or they might simply be a negative influence who's no good for me or who makes me feel 'less than'. If so, I'll use one or more of the techniques I mentioned in the section on family members. Other things I recommend include:

- **Notice whether the problem is situational.** If you've noticed that this friend is only negative in certain situations (for example, when you're drinking with them), try to find other things to do together.
- **Explain your decision to them.** If you feel you can't sort the issues out, but you still wish them the best, you might want to let them know why you're leaving their life. Just make sure you protect your energy and try to come from a place of love and compassion.
- **Simply walk away.** Alternatively, if you're happy to burn the bridge between you, just stop hanging out with them. Distance yourself from them, both in real life and online.
- **You could also do a nice 'parting ways' spell.** This can help you to both go your separate ways without leaving bad feelings between you. It can keep the energy between you at a high vibration. Try using the 'parting ways' spell on the following page.

Realise too that if you have mutual friends, letting go can be even harder. You have to prepare yourself for the possibility that when you let go of one friend, you might have to let go of all of them.

This happened to me and, although I'd prepared for it, it was still really hard. It felt like there was suddenly this big space in my life where they all used to be. What helped me through was using some of the tips above and spending more time with family members and friends who were positive, happy people.

Chapter 9: Your Circle

The other problem with distancing yourself from someone within your group of friends is that there are bound to be times where you run into each other. Although this can feel a little awkward, I've found that the best thing is to keep everything polite and positive. You don't need to go into your story then and there: just protect your energy, stay in your integrity and you'll be fine.

> Letting go is a beautiful act of self-love and ultimately of self-preservation.

I understand how challenging releasing people from your life can be. However, please believe me that letting go is a beautiful act of self-love and ultimately of self-preservation.

Your ritual work: a spell to part ways with love

Intention

To help you part ways with someone on good terms without anger, bitterness or resentment, while keeping your vibration and integrity high.

NOTE: You don't need the other person's permission to perform this spell. However, if the parting is mutual, you can ask them to be part of the spell.

Timing

Any, but a Waning Moon is the most energetically ideal.

You will need

- A smudge stick.
- All altar representations as per Chapter 2, including a white candle.

Wholistic Witchcraft

- A rose quartz crystal – in the shape of a heart if you can get it.
- A black moonstone to ease the grief of parting.
- A pink candle.
- One representation each of you and the person you're parting with. These can be photos or tokens.
- Two pictures of the Earth to represent you both going off into the world to do your own thing. You can either draw or print these pictures.
- A representation of Kuan Yin – the Chinese goddess of compassion, love, mercy and friendship. I usually use a Tarot or oracle card for this; but if you don't have one, you can print a picture off from the internet.

Ritual steps

1. Begin by preparing yourself and your sacred space.
2. Arrange all the tools you'll need for the ritual on your altar, or on a table or the floor.
3. Once you have everything set up, you might like to have a purification bath or shower as described in the rituals in previous chapters.
4. Smudge yourself, the space and all your tools and supplies.
5. Light the central, white altar candle, then cast a basic circle as you learnt to do in Chapter 2.
6. Call in the goddess Kuan Yin and ask for her guidance and blessing for your ritual.
7. Set out your altar as follows (see the diagram following this ritual):
   - Place the representations of yourself and the other person beside each other in the centre.
   - Place the rose quartz in the middle of the two representations.
   - Place the Kuan Yin representation above them.

Chapter 9: Your Circle

- Place the pictures of the Earth on either side of the personal representations, at the outer edges of your altar.
8. Light the pink candle.
9. Tune in to the energy of the other person, and imagine a bubble of pink unconditional love surrounding them. Speak the following chant:

*"I ask you to release me as I now release you
from the bonds of our ties.
In love I now send you forth to grow and evolve –
may you reach for the skies.
May the energy between us stay positive and true.
But for now, in this life, I must bid you adieu.
Merry we did meet, now merry we must part.
You will forever and always remain in my heart.
This is what I will, and it shall be so.
Blessed be and aho* (and so it is).*"*

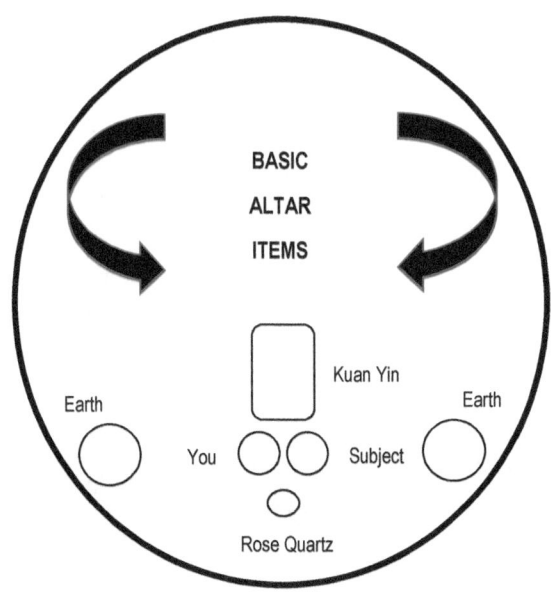

10. Now move the representations of you and the other person slightly apart towards the Earth pictures, leaving the rose quartz crystal and Kuan Yin in the centre.
11. Empower your moonstone crystal with your breath, asking it to help you through the grieving and parting process.
12. Close circle in the usual way (see Chapter 2), remembering to thank Kuan Yin.
13. Repeat the spell daily (including the chant) until both personal representations are resting on the pictures of the Earth. From the beginning of the spell, carry the moonstone crystal with you at all times until you feel the grief has eased or passed.

How to integrate these teachings into your wholistic lifestyle

Everyone will have a process that works best for them, and we're all made differently. That means it's really up to you to work out what will be best for your unique situation. You may like to get things done quickly (like cut someone off), or you may need more time to ease into it all. Either way, the tips below may help your process as they've often helped mine:

- **Awareness is key.** Start by just paying attention to who's around you and how you feel when you're with them. Journal about whatever you notice (see the 'Journal tasks' box below).
- **Who in your life is positive and happy?** Start spending more time with them.
- **Try to identify people who have a negative impact on your energy.** For each person, ask yourself what you need to do to remedy the situation. Do you need to distance yourself? Have a talk with them? Perform a ritual? Maybe some combination of these?

Chapter 9: Your Circle

- 🧙 **Get yourself a crystal to repel negative energy.** Try onyx, black tourmaline or obsidian. Wear it or keep it near you whenever you're around other people.
- 🧙 **Begin your day by surrounding yourself with a bubble of white light that no negative energies can infiltrate.** You may like to check in with it throughout the day to keep it nice and strong.
- 🧙 **Be really gentle with yourself.** There's no point in feeling angry, upset or ashamed for allowing negative people into your life. Everyone we meet is part of our journey and is always there to teach us something.
- 🧙 **Even when it's hard, try to always come from a place of compassion and love.** Sometimes, this is more for you than for the person in question – it keeps your vibration and integrity high.
- 🧙 **Really tune in to yourself and your feelings.** When you're thinking about releasing negative people, this can help you to avoid second-guessing yourself. It can reassure you that you're coming from a place of truth where others can't sway you into distrusting your own thinking and judgement.
- 🧙 **You might like to delete or silence people on social media.** It used to trigger me when I saw posts or stories from people online that I no longer wanted to be around, so I sometimes cut all ties. This is especially effective if the negative person is only a friend on Facebook or other social media.

If I don't want to actively unfriend someone, I'll just make them an 'acquaintance' so that I don't see their negative posts.

Book of Shadows

☽ Please record your ritual and the qualities of the crystals you used.

Journal tasks

🎩 Journal about who you surround yourself with. Think about whether you need to let go of any relationships — or alternatively, whether there are some you need to nurture more.
This extends to family, friends, co-workers, acquaintances or people in social groups you hang out in (yes, even online).

🎩 Journal your observations from your ritual.

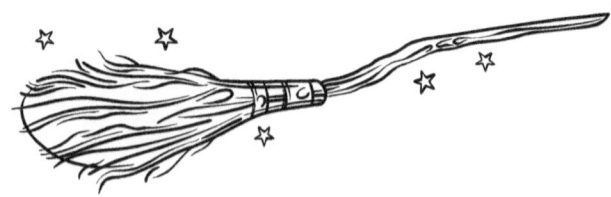

Chapter 9: Your Circle

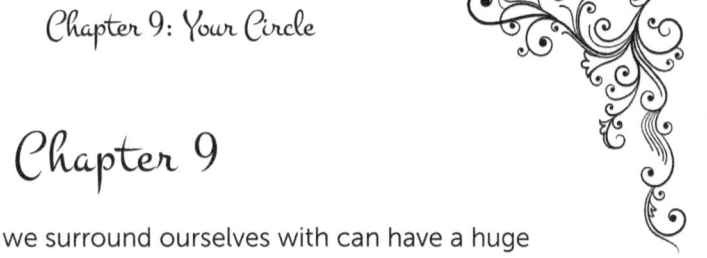

Summary - Chapter 9

- 🧙 The people we surround ourselves with can have a huge impact on our happiness, health and ability to grow spiritually.
- 🧙 Negative people who bring us down can drain our energy and make us question our worth.
- 🧙 On the other hand, supportive, positive people can lift us up and raise our vibrations.
- 🧙 If you currently have unsupportive, negative friends, family or acquaintances, consider reviewing your relationship and letting them go to make space for more positive, supportive people.
- 🧙 It's possible to release people from your life with love. You don't necessarily need to have an argument or burn a bridge to let go of someone.

Section 3

Spiralling Into Transformation

As the witchling has grown and evolved, she's discovered that not everything is sunshine, rainbows and lollipops. Yes, at times, she feels deliriously happy — but at others, she feels unexplainably melancholy and even sad. She laughs in delight at baby animals rolling around and playing, and feels intense anger at the cruelty of humans to each other and to the Earth.

As she begins to know herself on a deeper level, she starts to see patterns in her own cycles. She begins to understand her reactions and why she behaves as she does at times. She realises that no one can be closeted in a cave all their life and not carry some scarring from it!

So she turns now to the final leg of her path and sees that it's different to the one she's travelled so far. This path twists and turns. It's dark in places, and she can't see the way forward.

She knows she'll have to dig deep to face the fears she feels in the pit of her stomach and overcome them. At the same time, she understands that she must travel through this unknown terrain to reach her ultimate goal of stepping into her power.

Therefore, she turns to face it with bravery and determination.

Welcome to Section 3, dear one. Even though this section can be challenging and ask you to face things you've long buried or hidden, it's by far my favourite. Why? Because here is where you'll experience the most growth. In this section, you'll discover:

- the patterns you're holding onto that are keeping you from your power
- the hurts you've buried deep and refused to look at for fear of what they'll reveal
- the emotions you've been hiding from because they bring pain.

Some of these things you'll already know. You'll have uncovered them through your own life experiences and throughout your journey with this book. Others may come as a surprise.

In any case, in this section, you'll gain the information and support you need to unpack and transform anything you find into something that will empower you. You'll learn different healing techniques that you can call on at any moment.

You'll also embark on a shadow journey that will ultimately lead you to the light. And that light will be unlike anything you've ever experienced before, because you'll be experiencing it as a different person to the one who began this journey.

There's so much healing and transformation in this section for you, dear reader. And when you allow it to unfold as it's meant to, you'll ultimately shed the skin of your old Self. Underneath, you'll find what was always lying, waiting to be revealed: your truth and your power.

Now, more than ever, it's important to complete the practical tasks to allow yourself to experience this journey in all its fullness. Be brave. I promise that the effort is worth it, and I'm here for you in spirit to support and guide you.

Blessings

Bella x

CHAPTER 10
Healing

What is healing?

All of us, at some point in our lives, will have heard the term 'healing'. And many of us, especially as kids, have only ever thought of healing in terms of things like a sore knee getting better or recovering from an illness.

But healing happens on so much more than just a physical level. As evolved human beings, we can heal ourselves on an emotional and spiritual level too. In fact, healing ourselves emotionally or spiritually often leads naturally to physical healing.

> Healing happens on so much more than just a physical level.

This is why I view everything wholistically. I know that looking at the whole picture can reveal factors a client hasn't considered or discovered for themselves. And sometimes, the answer to healing can be much easier than they first thought.

A classic example is when a client comes to me for a facial and tells me that they struggle with bad skin. I'll always ask questions like:

- What products do you currently use?
- Have you been stressed lately?
- How's your diet?
- How much water are you drinking?

All of these factors combine to affect skin health and quality. So sometimes, simply drinking more water or eating less sugar can heal a skin issue without requiring medication.

We can heal ourselves wholistically in many different ways, utilising many different modalities. Finding the right one for you is a matter of doing your research and discovering what will work for you. This chapter aims to give you a 'leg up' on that research by sharing a snippet of what's out there and exploring how it can help you on your own healing journey.

Types of healing

Important disclaimer

Before we discuss healing in detail, it's essential to mention that Western medicine has its place. I am not *for one minute* recommending giving up your doctor-prescribed medication.

What I AM saying is that if you need prescribed medication, natural medicines and healing methods may help to make it more effective. They may also work well in conjunction with your meds to create more wholistic healing.

However, I strongly recommend speaking to a naturopath or other qualified healthcare professional before you start any new therapy. Some natural remedies can interact with your prescribed medications, either making them stronger, making them weaker or causing unpleasant – or even dangerous – side effects. So make sure you check anything you're thinking of taking internally with someone who knows what they're talking about!

Physical healing

If you aren't already using natural therapies to aid your physical healing, it might just be worth researching which ones could work for

Chapter 10: Healing

you. Personally, I'll always try natural healing before I agree to take medicine, and things have to be drastic for me to take meds. My favourite natural tools are:

- **wholesome food**, as per Chapter 1 – this is where it all starts: nutrition is everything
- **juices** – a way to concentrate the power of plant-based food and help give your digestion a rest without going short on nutrients
- **plant medicine** – using herbs and other plant ingredients for healing, such as using aloe vera for sunburn
- **essential oils** – the concentrated natural active compounds from within plants
- **potions** – liquid remedies that are useful to create healing and energetic shifts
- **natural salves and ointments** – external remedies in either solid or liquid form that you apply to your skin.

Other ways to use natural healing ingredients include:

- **poultices** – crushed up herbs and flowers mixed with a base oil to make a kind of paste, then applied to your skin
- **natural sprays** – herbs or essential oils added to water, vinegar, alcohol or some combination of the three in a spray bottle
- **herbal teas** – dried or fresh herbs steeped in boiling water that you drink
- **flower or herb essences** – flowers or herbs steeped in water or alcohol, usually for longer than for teas
- **hot and cold therapies** – a range of temperature-based therapies, including hot stone massage and hot/cold compresses.

You can find out more about each of these formats for healing (and all the techniques in the sections below) in books, online or by working with a mentor. See Appendix I for recommended book titles.

Emotional healing

Did you know that many physical ailments are associated with an emotion you're holding onto, which is negatively affecting your health? For more information on this, I highly recommend reading *The Secret Language of Your Body* (2007) by Inna Segal. This book explains what's at the core of illness and issues within the body, and the emotions attached to each one. (It also has a great section on colour therapy that I highly recommend.)

> Did you know that many physical ailments are associated with an emotion you're holding onto, which is negatively affecting your health?

For example, people who hold onto intense anger for a long time can develop cancers and other serious illnesses. Meanwhile, people who hold onto guilt and shame can develop physical ailments like a rash that will keep showing up until they release the emotion.

Owning and facing your emotional stuff isn't easy. On the other hand, staying stuck in the same place without changing or moving forward, and constantly feeling sick, sad, depressed or angry is a lot harder to bear.

I can't tell you exactly how much emotional healing I've done over the years, but it's a LOT. And I promise that the long-term benefits have far outweighed the moments of discomfort when I've been in the middle of owning my stuff. Emotional healing methods that I've tried and tested myself include:

- **journalling** – clearing your mind through writing
- **liquid crystals** – the essence of a crystal's energy in a liquid form that you can take internally
- **meditation** – the art of becoming present in the moment and quieting your mind
- **reiki** – a relaxing technique that harnesses healing, universal energy through the practitioner's palms

Chapter 10: Healing

- **shamanic healing** – a form of healing that addresses the root spiritual issues and causes of disease by working with energy, spirit guides and animal totems
- **EFT (Emotional Freedom Technique)** – the art of tapping meridian points to unblock and move energy around your body
- **Ho'oponopono** – a Hawaiian forgiveness technique
- **NLP (neuro-linguistic programming)** – reprogramming your brain with language
- **ThetaHealing** – a meditational process accessing the theta brainwave that creates physical, mental and spiritual healing through focused prayer to Creator or Deity.

With some of these techniques, I've experienced radical shifts and changes. With others, the healing has been more subtle or it hasn't seemed to do anything for me.

The most important thing is to just start. Try out different techniques to find out what feels right and true for you.

Spiritual healing

In both past lives and the one you're living now, I guarantee there've been times when your spirit has been hurt, injured and betrayed. These wounds can last for many lifetimes until they're finally healed.

In fact, over all these lifetimes, wounds can develop into patterns that begin to shape who you become. These patterns can influence what you believe and how you behave. For example, someone who lost a great love – whether in this life or a past one – can have issues letting anyone else in for fear of losing them again. Someone who was burnt at the stake in a past life may have trouble being open and honest about who they are for fear of being persecuted again.

Delving into and healing the core of these spiritual hurts can help you to release negative patterns, beliefs and behaviours that affect you in this life. I've experienced my biggest shifts through releasing shitty patterns using ThetaHealing and working with my chakras. Again, however, there are many, many modalities that can help you to experience the same thing.

Some of these include the meditation, shamanic journey work and NLP I mentioned above, plus:

> *Delving into and healing the core of spiritual hurts can help you to release negative patterns, beliefs and behaviours that affect you in this life.*

- 🧙 **chakra balancing** – energetically clearing and harmonising your chakras
- 🧙 **crystal healing** – using the energy and vibration of crystals to heal your mind, body and soul
- 🧙 **energy cleansing** – cleaning and clearing energy using energetic techniques
- 🧙 **past-life regression** – journeying into past lives to heal old wounds
- 🧙 **ritual** – this can encompass any kind of ritual for healing.

Take some time to explore these and other life-changing modalities to see which feels best for you.

🔮 Case study: a little tale of healing and magick...

Today, as I was preparing to sit down and write, I had the most magickal experience, which was the catalyst for self-healing to take place.

After finishing with a client, I walked out to my kitchen and a currawong appeared on my fence. He seemed to look me *straight* in the eye, then flew to a chair right in front of me. He

Chapter 10: Healing

proceeded to squawk his head off and shake his wings at me for a solid ten minutes, staring at me the whole time.

I didn't know whether this bird was distressed or maybe wanting to attack me, but I fed him some grapes and he calmed down. He even let me come sit next to him while he softly chirped before he went to sleep!

According to *Animal Dreaming* by Scott Alexander King (2007), the message of the Currawong is:

> Currawong supports us as we endeavour to reclaim our power and expel the weaker, more dependent aspects of our personality. It helps us face our inner demons – and depose them forever, while guiding us to unite our spiritual, mental and physical selves so that they may dance in harmony with one another instead of battling each other for supremacy.

Then, after this, I drew an oracle card, and got 'Letting Go'.

Coincidence? No, I think not.

Together, these two signs prompted me to explore what I needed to let go of. What came to me was that I was still holding onto who I WAS instead of accepting who I AM. I did some muscle testing around this and discovered that I held the belief that I didn't trust myself, which was why I couldn't accept myself.

Armed with this knowledge, I did some ThetaHealing to change the belief that I don't trust myself to one where 'I DO trust myself'. Changing this core belief rippled out to change a few other beliefs around this same subject, which in turn has helped me with self-acceptance

I still have more exploration and work to do, but today there's been a big shift for me that will help me to now move forward on my path.

I share this to demonstrate the power of healing and how dramatically it can change your life.

Ways to use these tools

While I *will* ask a mentor for help when I need to, I also constantly use self-healing techniques. This is easy to do if you have the right tools and resources to guide you. I regularly learn from books, listen to YouTube meditations and use various techniques I've learnt over the years. Let me share my favourites, and then please add your own to this list.

> While I *will* ask a mentor for help when I need to, I also constantly use self-healing techniques.

Chakra balancing

This technique balances and harmonises your chakras to bring your energy into alignment. It can be hugely beneficial on a physical, emotional and spiritual level.

To balance a chakra yourself, you can:

- meditate on it – for example, visualise it being open, clean and clear
- apply chakra-specific essential oil blends to the physical area the chakra sits in
- use its colour – for example, wear it, surround yourself with it or breathe it in
- use chakra crystals, which you can buy in sets.

Essential oils

I use various oils for myself and for my clients to invoke different types of healing. For example, I use:

- lavender oil for stress relief and relaxation
- lemon oil in my hot water first thing in the morning to flush my liver (be sure the brand you buy is suitable for internal use if you do this)

Chapter 10: Healing

- orange oil to regenerate energy and invoke a sense of wellbeing
- rose oil to bring in the energy of love.

I also use a grounding oil blend, a digestive healing blend and different chakra healing blends on an almost daily basis.

Journalling

I find journalling immensely healing and frequently prescribe it for my clients. It's a gentle but effective way to express your feelings, thoughts and emotions in a deeply personal way that's just for you.

Even if you're not normally a writer, I'd highly recommend getting yourself a beautiful journal to start recording your thoughts. It doesn't matter whether you write one word or a thousand, and it doesn't matter how you write. Just get everything out of your head and your body, thus releasing its energy and encouraging inner healing.

Liquid crystals

The list of things you can heal with liquid crystal essences is seriously unlimited. For example, I've used different essences to help me:

- feel protected while I was driving a long commute to work
- learn patience
- communicate more clearly and calmly
- assist me in a two-week shadow journey.

Jump online to find a practitioner in your area and learn more.

Magick sprays

I make my own sprays and am also blessed to have friends who make gorgeous sprays that I can use for many purposes, including healing. I regularly use:

- a sage smudge spray for cleansing
- a spray that's emotionally balancing

- another to work with my inner child
- a fourth that invokes unconditional love.

Have a squiz online to find sprays that resonate with you, or look up recipes to make your own.

Meditation

Meditation can be as simple as connecting with your breath to still yourself for a few moments, or it can take you on a deep journey within. Ways in which I use meditation include:

- calming my often-busy mind
- finding answers and gaining clarity
- healing
- relaxation
- ritual journeys
- relieving stress and anxiety.

I've been meditating for over 25 years and still find it hard to calm my mind at times. When this happens, I use guided meditations, which I get from books, CDs and YouTube.

Ritual

Rituals can be immensely healing when you design and perform them with strong intention. You can use ritual to heal yourself or people you love, as long as you ask their permission first.

If you want to perform a healing ritual, first think about the type of healing you wish to create. Is it physical, emotional or spiritual? Next, consider the outcome you'd like to achieve.

Then, choose some ritual tools, such as candles and crystals (see Appendix B for candle colour associations and Appendix C for crystal associations). You may also like to work with a particular healing deity and invoke them during your ritual. If so, research whoever you'd like to work with before you begin.

Chapter 10: Healing

And, finally, focus on either yourself or the person receiving the healing, and perhaps speak a chant or incantation.

See later in this chapter for a more specific example of a healing ritual.

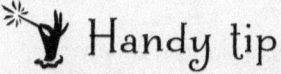 Handy tip

I encourage you to try even a few of these techniques to accelerate your journey on your path to wholistic health.

Bringing in a professional

While I use and recommend many self-healing techniques, sometimes with deep-seated issues, I can only go so far on my own. At those times, I need the help of a professional who can offer me a different perspective, a different energy and different techniques.

So let's take a closer, more in-depth look at some of the natural healing techniques offered by trained therapists.

> While I use and recommend many self-healing techniques, sometimes with deep-seated issues, I can only go so far on my own.

Access Bars

There are 32 points on your head known as 'bars', which store the electromagnetic components of your thoughts, blocked energy and stress. The Access Bars healing method involves gently touching these points to allow the charge on these areas to dissolve. This can then help to clear any limitations you're experiencing.

Some benefits of an Access Bars session include:

- better sleep
- less stress
- more energy
- weight loss
- easing of depression, and many more.

I've had an Access Bars session before and found it quite relaxing.

Crystal healing

Crystals can help to align, clear and transform your energy; different crystals each have different healing properties. Practitioners can place a crystal directly on your body wherever you need healing or ask you to wear it next to your skin for continuous healing benefits.

I've used crystals for years with great effect and either wear them in my bra, keep them next to my bed or put them in a necklace. Professionals can also create a crystal grid for you for a specific purpose, or place one or more crystals in water for you to drink as an elixir.

EFT (Emotional Freedom Technique)

This technique releases the energy of negative, trapped emotions that you've been holding onto. Beyond pure emotional healing, its benefits can include healing:

- addictions
- disorders
- phobias
- physical conditions, including chronic pain and disease
- PTSD (post-traumatic stress disorder).

EFT is a fairly simple technique that I've personally used with great success to help me change a negative mindset.

Chapter 10: Healing

Liquid crystals

We talked about these remedies in the previous section: they're made up of minerals, metals and crystals from Mother Earth. Practitioners create them by reproducing the energetic healing properties of a stone and replicating its internal geometry. This means the crystal can continue living as a liquid – amazing, really!

I've taken many liquid crystal remedies, as I mentioned earlier in the chapter. In every case, I've had amazing – and *permanent* – results, so I highly recommend them.

Reiki

Even if you've been attuned to reiki yourself, you'll sometimes get better results from working with another professional. Benefits of reiki include:

- physical healing
- reduced stress
- relaxation
- feelings of peace, security and overall wellbeing.

I've had several reiki treatments and found them quite gentle and relaxing.

Shamanic healing

Shamans believe that all healing is self-healing. So while they can communicate with spirit guides and move energy around your body, you ultimately have to be ready to do the work to heal yourself.

You'll usually experience a session with a trained shamanic healer as a gentle energy clearing or regeneration. The shaman will first reach a shamanic state of consciousness using rattles or drums to connect with their spirit guide team. Then they'll use one or more healing techniques such as:

- divination
- drum healing
- energetic healing
- shamanic doctoring
- soul or power animal retrieval.

These techniques are each aimed to either help you heal directly, or to help you find answers about your purpose in life and what you need to heal.

ThetaHealing

Theta is a state in which you have the power to change and create your reality instantly. This means you can:

- manifest what you need
- remove trauma or nasty entities that are sucking your energy
- retrieve soul fragments you've given away to others
- send unconditional love
- transform negative belief patterns... and so much more.

I'm a trained ThetaHealing practitioner myself. I was moved to study this amazing modality after experiencing healing sessions that created major shifts for me.

Handy tip

This is only a small snippet of the thousands of natural healing modalities available. I'd recommend doing more of your own research to find what will best work and resonate for you.

Chapter 10: Healing

Your ritual work: a healing spell

Intention

To heal or help to heal physical, emotional or spiritual ailments.

Please note: if you're performing this healing ritual for another person, first ask their permission. Their higher self may not allow the healing if they're not ready for it. If they give you permission, focus your intention and visualisations on them during the ritual steps.

Timing

Any. However, perform the spell during the Waning Moon to take illness away, or during the Waxing Moon to speed up healing.

You will need

- Four white candles to mark the directions.
- Representations of each of the elements and the Goddess and God for your altar as per Chapter 2.
- An amethyst crystal.
- A blue candle.
- A white candle.
- A picture of Panacea – the Greek goddess of healing any ailment (print one off the internet).
- A smudge stick.
- A lighter.

Ritual steps

1. Find a private space where you won't be disturbed.
2. Gather the tools you'll need and place them on or around your altar.

3. Use the smudge stick to cleanse yourself, your circle and all the items you'll use for your ritual.
4. Cast the simple circle you learnt in Chapter 2, and invoke the goddess Panacea as you do.
5. Light the blue candle, then close your eyes and breathe deeply for a few moments, thinking about the purpose of your spell.
6. Perform a scan to get a better sense of what needs healing:
   - For physical healing, scan your (or your subject's) body from head to toe, and notice any areas of pain or discomfort.

     I imagine that I'm going into my (or my subject's) body with a torch that lights up any problem areas, which may appear as a shadow or unhealthy flesh.
   - For emotional healing, tune in and notice any emotions that you or your subject are struggling with.
   - For spiritual healing, tune in and notice the areas where you feel spiritually disconnected.
7. Open your eyes, light the white candle, and stare at the light it emits for a minute.
8. Lie down within the circle, then close your eyes again and ask the goddess Panacea to bless you or your subject with the healing needed. Relax and allow whatever visions or feelings come over you to flow. Just trust that the healing is happening.

   When I ask for healing for myself, I often envision it as a white/gold shower that gently falls over me. I absorb the energy into myself, sending it where it needs to go. Sometimes I feel a tingling sensation too, but your experience will be your own.
9. When you feel the healing is complete, open your eyes and sit up. At this point, you might like to empower your crystal with a command or a chant relevant to the healing that has taken place. For example:

   "Help keep my heart beating strong and in good health."
10. Blow or snuff out your candles, and thank the goddess Panacea for her healing.

Chapter 10: Healing

11. Keep the amethyst crystal on you to help the healing continue after your ritual is complete. If you've completed this ritual for someone else, you may like to send them the crystal or keep it next to a photo of them.
12. Close the circle in the usual way, as you learnt in Chapter 2.

How to integrate these teachings into your wholistic lifestyle

- 🧙 **The first thing I'd say is that if you've never done healing before, just start.** Don't be afraid that you'll do things 'wrong'. Any healing method you try will benefit you in some way.

    NOTE: The exception to this rule is if you're planning to use products topically or internally. In that case, it's important to know what you're doing and/or check with a professional.

- 🧙 **Pick one of the self-healing techniques above and give it a go.** There are a gazillion books on specific healing modalities, as well as YouTube videos you can watch to help.

- 🧙 **If you already dabble in the healing arts, try something different and see whether you get different results.** Sometimes, dealing with an issue in a different way has given me a totally different perspective. This then usually leads me on a wonderous new path of healing and growth.

- 🧙 **I'd also recommend visiting a professional healer if you need more help.** For example, you might need advice, guidance or help with something you're having trouble with yourself.

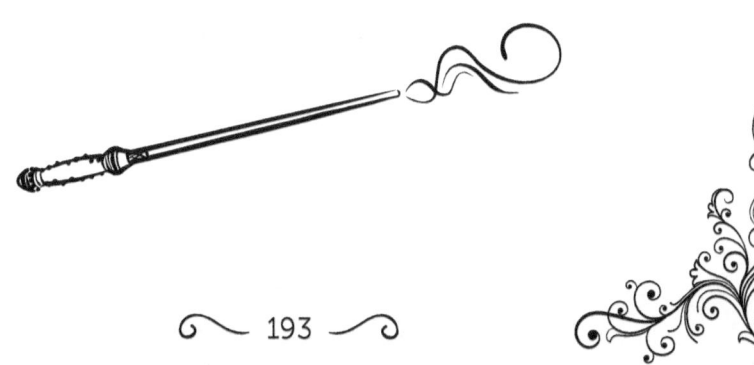

Book of Shadows

☽ Please record your ritual and the qualities of the crystal used.

☽ You might also like to record each of the different types of healing mentioned above. Perhaps you could do some more research into the ones that interest you and make notes on what you discover.

Journal tasks

🎩 Please journal your observations from the ritual.

🎩 Please also journal any healings you do or experience after reading this chapter, plus any outcomes. This can help you to gain clarity around what you need to do next.

Chapter 10: Healing

Summary - Chapter 10

- We tend to think of healing as purely physical, but it can also occur on an emotional and spiritual level.
- For best results, it's always a good idea to look at everything from a wholistic point of view.
- There's a wide variety of healing tools available – some you can practise on your own, and others you'll need to speak with a professional about.
- Healing works in different ways for different people, and what works for one person may not work for you – so doing your research is essential.
- If you're on prescribed medication, always check with your healthcare professional before you take any products to make sure they won't affect your medication.

CHAPTER 11
Love Thyself

> **Remember**
> You are a part of the Moon, the Stars, the Earth and the Universe, and therefore you are magnificent just as you are.

I believe that this is one of the most important chapters in this book. Why? Because on my own journey to wholeness, I've discovered that love – and in particular, self-love – is the answer to everything.

> Love – and in particular, self-love – is the answer to everything.

It took me a long time to understand this, and I've had times when my self-esteem has taken a blow. For example, people have commented negatively on my figure, compared me or what I do to someone who's doing better, or lashed out at me.

All of these things have triggered feelings of low worth, insecurity and not being accepted. Sometimes, I've wallowed in it for a week or more. Eventually, however, I've realised that this is when I most need to smother myself with love, care and nurturing to reconnect with who I really am.

As my awareness of what triggers me has grown, I've worked hard to heal my self-love, self-acceptance and self-worth. And as I've healed,

I've found that these aspects have all strengthened greatly within me. This has then helped me to evolve personally and magickally.

As a result, I trust and believe in myself more now. This means I can be freer and trust in the process more when I'm making a change in my life or performing a ritual. It has also:

- improved my relationships
- helped me to treat my body better
- given me the confidence to say 'yes' to more things
- helped me to believe in myself enough to keep going with my business.

While this work can be confronting at times, it's absolutely invaluable.

What IS self-love?

What does it mean to truly love yourself?

At its core, self-love is about your relationship with yourself. I believe that true self-love is a feeling that goes all the way down into your bones. It means accepting and understanding that your value and your worth goes far beyond:

- how you see yourself in the mirror
- how much money you have
- how others see you.

> Self-love means accepting all the pieces of your mind, body and soul – flaws and all – and understanding that you are, in fact, a divine being.

Self-love means accepting all the pieces of your mind, body and soul – flaws and all – and understanding that you are, in fact, a divine being.

When you love and accept yourself on every level, you can express yourself from a place of truth and integrity because you are the

Chapter 11: Love Thyself

'you-est' version of you. Your words, thoughts and deeds are authentic, so you rarely – if ever – doubt or question yourself. Instead, you make the best decisions for your highest self and those in your circle.

In short, you're someone who lives in your power, which means you've mastered the art of weaving magick throughout your everyday life. As such, your rituals, spells and daily personal practices are filled with pure intent, giving everything you do the best likely successful outcome.

Of course, it's my dearest hope that this description reflects you to a 'T'... but I know through my own experiences that it's just not the case for most of us. Many of us carry blocks to self-love due to factors such as:

- abuse
- beliefs
- familial patterns
- genetics
- past-life karma
- social conditioning.

These blocks can then manifest as:

- bad relationships
- eating disorders
- lack of self-care
- low self-esteem
- using sex to numb out, or the opposite – fearing intimacy
- rollercoaster emotions
- self-abuse
- the tendency to put everyone else's needs first.

Begin the journey to loving you

So how do you bring in more feelings of self-love and break the chains that hold you back from true self-acceptance? What will free you and allow you to give and receive unconditional love? What will help you to step into your power?

Below is a list of the techniques that have helped me in the past. They also continue to help me if I need a self-love injection to reconnect with my power – because, let's face it, we're all constantly healing and evolving. I invite you to try one, a few, or all of them:

- **Notice your existing self-talk:** if you discover that it's negative, reframe your language. Negative self-talk can actively lower your vibration and is harmful for your emotional health. This was a big game-changer for me.
- **Journalling:** investigate and identify what your beliefs about yourself actually are. Once you've done that, you can begin the path to healing.
- **Meditation:** I'd recommend finding a heart chakra meditation on YouTube to begin opening and harmonising this chakra. Remember: This is your centre of unconditional love.
- **Pampering:** look at ways to practise self-care for your mind, body and soul. Begin with small daily acts of kindness to yourself to help chip away at those barriers you've built up against self-love.
- **Ritual:** I've often used ritual to help me remove self-love blocks. I usually design my own ritual, basing it completely intuitively on what my mind, body and soul need at the time. This includes the tools I need to use and the words I need to say.

  I believe that unplanned rituals based purely on instinct and feeling are often the best ones, because your intentions during them are often far more powerful.
- **Self-healing:** use one or more of the self-healing techniques we discussed in Chapter 10. Reread that information and pick

Chapter 11: Love Thyself

a technique that calls to you. Reach out to work with a professional therapist if you need extra help in shifting unloving beliefs about yourself.

Your ritual work: taking a spiritual retreat

This ritual is a full day of magick just for you and is designed to help you recharge, rebalance and reconnect.

Recently, at the end of a very busy month that had me feeling disconnected, grumpy and uninspired, I took one of these for myself and it was AH-mazing. It totally got me back to where I needed to be, so I encourage you to make the space to give yourself this loving gift.

The most important thing with this ritual is that you tailor it to whatever will nourish you best. I've shared what I did below as a guide only.

Intention

To take time out to reconnect with yourself, experience self-love, explore your innermost desires, discover more about yourself, and reset and rebalance.

Timing

Any, but most potent during a Waxing Moon.

You will need

- Representations of each of the elements and the Goddess and God for your altar, as per previous chapters.
- A smudge stick.
- A lighter.
- Salt.

Wholistic Witchcraft

- Cleansing and/or protective incense. I use powdered incense that I've made myself to burn with charcoal discs. (Plus charcoal discs if you also use powdered incense.)
- Tarot and/or oracle cards. You might also like to use other divinatory tools such as runes or a pendulum.
- A chakra balancing meditation. If you haven't done one before, I'd recommend downloading mine (see the link in Appendix I) or find one on YouTube. Have this meditation ready before you start the ritual.
- Something you can listen to the meditation on. I used my phone (switched to silent).
- A grounding oil blend – I recommend doTERRA Balance and use it almost daily.
- A journal or paper and pen.
- Anything else that feels good to you to include. For example, on my altar during my retreat, I also had:
  - flowers and greenery from my garden
  - my mini-cauldron to burn powdered incense
  - my athame to cast the circle
  - chakra oils
  - a large obsidian crystal (for true self-reflection)

Ritual steps

1. Find a private space where you won't be disturbed.
2. Gather the tools you'll need and place them on or around your altar.
3. Cleanse yourself in the same way you've done for previous rituals.
4. Use the smudge stick to cleanse yourself, your sacred space and all the items you'll use for your ritual.
5. Cast the simple circle as you learnt in Chapter 2.
6. Sit before your altar and spend a few minutes focusing on your intention for what you're going to do today.

Chapter 11: Love Thyself

7. Start by balancing your chakras, using the meditation you chose during your preparation.

   For my ritual, I went through each chakra, starting at my base chakra. I applied the appropriate essential oil blend to the area over each chakra, then breathed in its colour. Finally, I focused on it until it felt energised and radiant.

8. Now apply your grounding oil. I usually apply mine to the back of my neck, but you can use yours wherever you intuitively feel is best. Close your eyes and spend a minute connecting with the Goddess and God. Ask them (again) to watch over and protect you during your rite today. Also ask them for anything else you think you may need, such as clarity or guidance.

9. Give your gratitude to the Universe for all the blessings in your life. You might like to meditate on them, declare them out loud or write them in your journal.

10. Draw an oracle card for general guidance today.

11. Give yourself a more in-depth Tarot reading in the same way you did in Chapter 6. I did mine for 12 months, but you could do yours for whatever time period feels appropriate.

12. Journal each step of your ritual as you go, including details about the reading.

13. When you feel complete, close circle in the usual way as you learnt in Chapter 2.

Additional notes/suggestions

- It's a good idea to speak to your family and ask for space and privacy before you start this ritual. Also, keep your phone on silent all day, and don't engage with it except to listen to the meditation/s.

> Speak to your family and ask for space and privacy before you start this ritual.

- You may want to do a 'shadow meditation' (more about shadow work in the next chapter) as part of your ritual. For example, if you're feeling irritable, this can help you to see the 'shadow' of your situation and why you're feeling that way.

It can also show you what you need to let go of and what you need to look at that is no longer serving you. This then gives you insight into what you might need to transform or heal in the future.

- Then, based on your insights from the reading or the shadow meditation (if you did one), you might like to do some healing work. Refer to Chapter 10 for a comprehensive list of modalities.
- As you go through your day, try to work really intuitively. Actively feel into what you most need in every moment.
- I'm usually a gym-goer. However, when I do this kind of retreat, I prefer to exercise more gently, eg. with 20 minutes of yoga towards the end of the retreat.
- Nourish yourself with really good, clean food all day. Then go to bed nice and early and do your best to get an excellent night's sleep.

How to integrate these teachings into your wholistic lifestyle

Begin with small, daily acts of kindness that bring pleasure to your mind, body and soul. These will help to raise your vibration, giving you a greater sense of wellbeing. Over time, this will lead to more feelings of love and more acceptance. Here are a few of my favourites:

> Begin with small, daily acts of kindness that bring pleasure to your mind, body and soul.

- **Nourish your body with clean, wholesome food.** Seriously, I know I bang on about this, but there's no better gift to yourself!

Chapter 11: Love Thyself

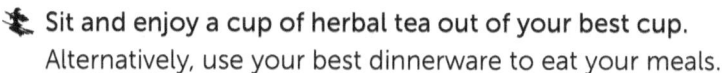

- Sit and enjoy a cup of herbal tea out of your best cup. Alternatively, use your best dinnerware to eat your meals.
- Every morning, look deep into your own eyes in the mirror and say, "I love you." This may feel silly or difficult at first, but please believe me that it can help create big shifts.
- Read or listen to something that expands your mind. You can find some great resources in Appendix I that will open you up to new possibilities.
- Take a little extra time and care when you get ready in the morning. Give yourself a bit of pampering and put some effort into your presentation. Why not dress up every day? I believe life's too short not to! You're not doing this for others – it's purely for you and how you feel about yourself.
- Move your body at least three times a week. This helps to keep your skin taut and your health in tip-top condition. But most importantly, it creates endorphins (feel-good brain chemicals) that make you feel great about yourself!
- Prepare a bath for yourself. Enjoy it with candles and a good book – and a glass of wine is pretty nice too!
- Create sacred spaces around your home. Go back to Chapter 7 for specific ideas on this. But also realise that even something as simple as buying or cutting yourself fresh flowers and placing them where you'll constantly see them can really lift your vibration.
- Draw an oracle card each day for guidance. Alternatively, you can give yourself a daily Tarot reading.
- Get out in Nature regularly. Why not sit under a tree and daydream? Or you could hang out with animals: they're so full of love and can often lift your mood.

Book of Shadows

☽ Please record your ritual – at least the main elements of it – so you can refer back to it when you need some self-loving.

☽ You might also like to record correspondences to love – crystals, deities, colours, etc. (check the Appendices for guidance).

🪶 Journal tasks

There are a few journal tasks in this chapter, and I believe they're all an important part of your evolution to living a wholistic lifestyle.

🧙 First of all, meditate for a few minutes on what your beliefs are about yourself – dig deep and be really honest. Record your findings.

🧙 Also record any observations from any of the healing techniques you try.

🧙 Journal every step of your ritual, and later, add reflections. For my ritual, I wrote out my steps straight afterwards, then slept on it and added in my reflections the next day.

🧙 Please also journal your current answers to the following statements. These statements cover similar content to the quiz you did in Chapter 1, but reviewing these now will help you see how far you have come since the

Chapter 11: Love Thyself

beginning of your journey. As I'm sure you've realised by now, every one of these practices is, in fact, an act of self-love.

- I nourish my body with nutritious, clean food every day.
- I drink a minimum of two litres of water every day.
- I get a minimum of seven hours of sleep each night.
- I move my body for a minimum of 30 minutes at least three times a week.
- I have a handle on drugs, tobacco and alcohol.
- I nourish my soul every day with one or more of the following: daily ritual, card readings, meditation, healing or whatever nourishes me.
- I enjoy healthy, uplifting relationships with my family and friends.
- I have a good work/life balance.

Give yourself a score out of 10 for each statement to identify where you may need to give more energy to your self-love rituals. Again, if you score below 5, you need to give that area lots more energy. Scoring between 5 to 7 means you could give a bit more energy to this area. If you score 8 or above, you're doing great – keep going!

◂ Finally, please journal any healings you do or experience after reading this chapter, plus any outcomes. Again, this can help you to gain clarity around what you need to do next.

Summary - Chapter 11

- 🧙 Loving yourself at the deepest possible level is the key to everything in wholistic witchcraft.
- 🧙 When you love yourself fully, you're in your power, which means you're powerful.
- 🧙 Journalling, meditation, ritual, and investigating and changing your self-talk can all be powerful practices for increasing self-love.
- 🧙 If you identify any blocks to self-love, there are ways to diminish them and create space for more love in your life.
- 🧙 Small daily acts of kindness to yourself can create big shifts.

CHAPTER 12
Journey to Shadow

What is shadow work?

Shadow work, shadow journeys, working with your dark side, dwelling in the Underworld... I'd never even *heard* of shadow work until a couple of years ago. It turned out, however, that I'd already been doing it for a long time. It's just that the kind of deep, healing ritual work I'd been practising suddenly had a name.

Now I seem to hear about it constantly.

The thing is that shadow work isn't just a fad or the latest trend – it's serious stuff that's incredibly valuable for growth and evolution. But what *is* it exactly?

Shadow work is essentially about looking deeply at what you perceive as the darker or more negative aspects of your personality. And, if you need to, it's about healing or transforming those traits into something that can work for you more positively.

> Shadow work isn't just a fad or the latest trend – it's serious stuff that's incredibly valuable for growth and evolution.

Think it as being a bit like peeling away the layers of an onion. In shadow work, however, each 'layer' is a mask or a veil that you've constructed around a truth to hide from it. So each layer you peel away brings you a step closer to your truth.

A shadow journey can last for an hour, a day, a week, months or even a year; and it will be a totally different experience each and every time.

The benefits of shadow work

If you're interested in evolving into the best version of yourself (which I'm guessing you are because you're reading this book), shadow work is a wonderful tool. Using it will help you to grow in ways – and to a level – that you've never experienced before.

There are many (so, so many) people in our society who suffer from maladies like:

- anger
- depression
- egotism
- general unpleasantness
- judgement
- meanness
- narcissism
- sadness
- self-righteousness
- single-mindedness.

Actually, for some of those people, I say they 'suffer', but it's more likely that the people around them suffer. They, on the other hand, are quite happy being the way they are.

But many other people (and you may be one of these) are aware that their behaviour isn't serving them and their highest good. They don't want to be that way... so they know they need to make some changes.

If you're one of those people, here are just a few of the benefits of shadow journeys:

- being able to speak your truth
- enjoying a healthier relationship with both yourself and others
- feeling more confident and authentic
- healing old wounds, which leads to more balanced emotions

Chapter 12: Journey to Shadow

- knowing yourself in a deeper way and building your self-trust
- strengthening your intuition and your connection with yourself and the Divine.

Case study: how shadow work changed my life

For the longest time, I had a real problem with being judged. It made my skin crawl, and I'd feel myself getting angry. And 20 years ago, because my husband and I both looked very 'different' (as in total goths), we got looked at a lot.

For some reason, I believed that *everyone* was negatively judging us... right up until the day I caught a bloke openly staring at me. I could feel the anger starting to rise, and I looked him straight in the eye and demanded, "What the hell are YOU looking at?"

I'll never forget his response: "You! You're magnificent!"

Oh dang... talk about awkward.

From that moment, my perception of judgement began to change. I also began to grow aware of how I myself was judging others. It turned out that I could be quite a nasty little witch in my head!

Over the years since then, I've done a lot of work on my tendency to negatively judge. I've healed what needed to be healed and found better ways to use my judgement. For example, being a better judge of character helps me to avoid negative engagements with others. Judging situations fairly also helps me to avoid making unfair assumptions and creating unnecessary dramas.

Judgement in its negative aspect was one of my shadows. Discovering and then healing that judgement is a perfect example of what shadow work is all about.

An important warning about shadow work

Before we continue, I need to tell you upfront: **shadow work is not for the faint-hearted.**

> Shadow work is not for the faint-hearted.

Nor is it a good idea if you're already struggling with anything mentally or emotionally.

In fact, it's absolutely vital to be mentally and emotionally sound before you begin any sort of shadow work. If you're currently on any medication for anxiety, depression or mental illness, please DON'T try any shadow work unless it's under the care of a qualified professional. Even then, I recommend extreme caution.

So before you start, please make sure you can check off the following:

- You're mentally healthy, including not currently suffering from anxiety or depression.
- You're not currently on any medication that makes your brain foggy.
- You're confident and experienced in ritual.
- You're highly in tune with, and aware of, yourself.
- Because you're highly aware of yourself, you know you can pull yourself out of a shadow journey when it's time.
- You're happy to seek the help of a mentor or healer after the shadow journey if you need to.
- You're willing to keep your energy high by using excellent self-care throughout your journey.

Chapter 12: Journey to Shadow

How to work with your shadow

Shadow work starts with noticing

Let's say you're good to go and you can say 'Yes' to all of the previous points. How can you then become aware of your shadows?

Start by noticing any negative or unhelpful feelings or behaviours within yourself, such as:

- behaviours that aren't for your highest good, like:
  - addictions
  - being unforgiving
  - holding grudges
  - lashing out at others in anger
  - being nasty or spiteful
  - resenting others for your life
- blaming everyone else for your life or situation instead of taking responsibility for it
- creating drama for yourself or those around you
- experiencing a lot of negative feelings, such as:
  - anger
  - anxiety
  - depression
  - fear
  - sadness
  - social awkwardness or anxiety
- only listening to your own point of view and believing that it's the only one that can be right
- reacting badly to 'normal' situations and not being able to solve problems or deal with challenges
- sitting in your comfort zone and refusing to change

- struggling to be happy for others who are doing well because you're envious or jealous.

The next step is questioning

Once you're more aware of your own negative behaviours, you can start asking yourself:

- How do I feel about myself?
- What are my exchanges with others like?
- What aspects of my personality are holding me back?
- What am I afraid of?

Now, make no mistake – this is confronting stuff! It definitely requires a good dose of courage to look at yourself this intimately and ask these hard questions. Believe me, though: doing this work of your own accord is infinitely better than having to do it because someone else has brought your negative behaviours to your attention.

For example, when we first got together, my husband told me I was selfish. I remember being SO offended – how dare he? But later, I thought about his comment and realised that, in a lot of ways, I totally was.

> Doing this work of your own accord is infinitely better than having to do it because someone else has brought your negative behaviours to your attention.

I also realised that my behaviour was a defence mechanism I'd created after experiencing trauma in a previous relationship.

I knew it wasn't fair for me to bring that coping mechanism into my new relationship. That meant I needed to change my selfish behaviours into more positive ones that benefited both me and everyone around me.

So I started to practise being more kind, considerate, compassionate and sharing. (At least with some things. Chocolate is still sacred!)

Chapter 12: Journey to Shadow

You might not be ready for this part of the journey just yet

Based on what I've said above, you may decide that shadow work isn't for you right now. If so, that's 100% OK. The only thing I'll say is that if you're already aware of some of your shadow aspects, they'll keep coming up to bite you until you're ready to deal with them. They'll show themselves as unpleasant feelings, dramas in your life, negative exchanges with others and, sometimes, just staying stagnant and stuck in one place.

> If you're already aware of some of your shadow aspects, they'll keep coming up to bite you until you're ready to deal with them.

As I keep saying, your journey is your own. So if and when you're ready, I'd recommend starting slowly and gently. Perhaps try one (and only one – more could be overwhelming) of these techniques to begin with:

- **Journal – let it alllll out.** Journal everything you're currently feeling – good and bad.
- **Do some healing processes from one of the books in Appendix I (or from Chapter 10).** I did several healing processes around judgement, for example. It's a nice, gentle way to begin clearing the energy.
- **If your shadows are hidden, I'd recommend a short guided shadow meditation to reveal them.** I suggest using my creation *Journey to the Underworld for Transformation* (see Appendix I). I've used it many times for both myself and my clients, and it's helpful for seeing whatever you need to see.

   Alternatively, you can find plenty of meditations on this topic on YouTube.
- **Work with a mentor or healer to help guide you.** Especially when you're working at this deep a level, it can be vital to reach out for help when you need it.

- 🜚 **Do a simple ritual working with the gods or goddesses of the Underworld.** Ask them to reveal to you what needs to be seen, and then ask them to help guide you through whatever you discover.

- 🜚 **Use your divination tools and ask them pointed questions.** Try asking, "What shadow aspect do I need to work with right now?" You could also incorporate this technique into your ritual.

Once you have a feel for the work you're doing and are experiencing the healing benefits, you might like to go deeper. If so, I encourage you to do so because, as you continue to grow and evolve, you're stepping into the fullness of yourself. As such, you're stepping into the best possible version of you.

I've taken quite a few shadow journeys now. In fact, I'm in a two-week Waning-to-Dark Moon shadow journey as I write this chapter. And even at this point, I can tell you that I've never felt more confident or more authentic than I do now.

This work has been truly magickal for me.

Take your time

One thing that's super important is that you must allow time between journeys to integrate the healing you've done.

Quite often, you'll build new neural pathways as your brain trains to become the new version of you. You need to allow those pathways time to form. Sometimes, I take a few weeks between journeys, and sometimes I take months.

> You must allow time between journeys to integrate the healing you've done.

🜚 You'll know when the time is right to move on.

Chapter 12: Journey to Shadow

To go deeper, you may do richer meditations or more involved rituals. You may also choose to work with someone who really brings your 'stuff' out of you. But no matter *how* much shadow work you've done, it never (like ever!) ceases to be confronting.

That means it's super-*mega*-important to equip yourself well with the tools and knowledge you need to get the most from your journeys without putting yourself in danger.

Pre-ritual journal tasks

Before you perform the ritual below, please complete these journal tasks.

- Begin by journalling how you're feeling right now — both the good and bad.
- Journal your answers to these questions:
    - How do I feel about myself?
    - What are my exchanges with others like?
    - What aspects of my personality are actually holding me back?
    - What am I afraid of?

Once you've journaled your answers to these questions, you're ready to begin your ritual.

Your ritual work: a gentle journey to the Shadowlands

Intentions

To discover what your shadows are, shed light on the one you need to work with right now, and learn what needs to be healed or transformed.

Timing

Any time between the first Waning Moon and the Dark Moon.

You will need

- Representations of each of the elements and the Goddess and God for your altar (refer to previous chapters).
- A smudge stick.
- A lighter.
- Salt.
- Cleansing or protective incense (or both). As I mentioned in Chapter 11, I burn powdered incense that I've made myself to use with charcoal discs.

  (Again, plus charcoal discs if you're also going with powdered incense.)
- A Tarot card or other image of the goddess Inanna. You can print one off the internet if you don't have one on hand.
- A black obsidian crystal.
- A deck of Tarot or oracle cards or both.
- A shadow journey meditation. Use my *Journey to the Underworld for Transformation* meditation (see Appendix I) or find one on YouTube.

Chapter 12: Journey to Shadow

- 🧙 Something you can listen to the meditation on. I use my phone (set on silent!)
- 🧙 Your journal or paper and pen.

Ritual steps

1. Find a private space where you won't be disturbed.
2. Gather the tools you'll need, and place them on or around your altar.
3. Cleanse yourself in the same way you've done for previous rituals.
4. Use your smudge stick to cleanse your sacred space and all the items you'll use for your ritual.
5. Place the Tarot card or image of Inanna and the obsidian crystal on your altar (anywhere that feels right).
6. Cast a simple circle as per Chapter 2, calling in the goddess Inanna and asking her to guide your journey.
7. Sit before your altar and spend a few minutes quieting your mind. Focus your intention on what you're going to do today.
8. Shuffle your oracle or Tarot deck and draw three cards, asking these questions as you do so:
    - **Card 1**: What shadow aspect do I need to release?
    - **Card 2**: What shadow aspect do I need to focus on right now?
    - **Card 3**: What shadow aspect am I not seeing that I need to bring to the light?
9. At this point, I recommend doing your shadow meditation to focus on releasing whatever you've discovered you need to release.
10. After your meditation, speak these words into your obsidian crystal:

"Keep revealing to me,
the truth of what I need to see,
so that my shadows can be healed and free."

Carry the crystal on you at all times or whenever you feel it's appropriate.

11. Close your circle in the usual way (see Chapter 2), making sure to give thanks to Inanna as you do.

How to integrate these teachings into your wholistic lifestyle

- Begin by noticing your thoughts and behaviours more. Are they serving your highest good? Notice also:
  - how you react to change
  - how you feel in social situations
  - your reactions to people and things.
- Journal, journal, journal! It's one of THE most powerful tools for self-awareness and transformation.
- Begin with self-guided gentle meditations. Close your eyes, relax, try to empty your mind and see where it takes you.
- Pull an oracle or Tarot card when it feels right to. Ask, "What shadow aspect of myself is ready to be revealed?" to get a starting point to work with.
- Begin to turn negative behaviours and thoughts into positive ones. This may take a lot of practice, but stick with it!

Book of Shadows

☽ Record your ritual and your observations.

☽ Do some research on the gods and goddesses of the Underworld and record your findings.

Chapter 12: Journey to Shadow

✒ Journal tasks

🎩 Journal what you've discovered about yourself from the questions above, and begin mapping out your own shadow journey (only if you're ready to, of course).

🎩 Journal your observations from your card readings or meditations.

🎩 Journal your observations from the ritual.

Summary - Chapter 12

- 🧙 Shadow work involves exploring the darker aspects of your personality, and then healing or transforming them.
- 🧙 It can be a life-changing practice with benefits that include healing old negative beliefs and behaviours that have been hindering you.
- 🧙 However, it can be dangerous if you're unprepared, or in a state of mental or emotional imbalance, so I always recommend caution.
- 🧙 Ritual and meditation are excellent ways to discover what your shadows are if you don't already know.
- 🧙 It's important to rest between shadow journeys to allow time for the healing that has taken place to integrate.

CHAPTER 13

Reclaiming Your Power

Reclaiming your power is the most magickal experience

I'll openly tell you that I've had some challenges as I've been writing this book. Some chapters have flowed along beautifully and almost felt like they wrote themselves. Others, however, have had me feeling stuck for weeks.

As I stated in the beginning, this whole book is based on my own experiences. I've fully lived every part of it. And it's been quite interesting to discover that I still had my own healing to do in places – particularly around self-love and power.

The Universe threw some pretty enormous challenges at me during writing that forced me to dig really deep. Those challenges brought up several remaining negative beliefs and patterns of behaviour that I didn't realise were still blocking me.

So believe me when I tell you that I've been taking this journey along with you all the way. And now, here, right at the end, it feels magickal to step into the fullness of my power.

I've experienced amazing moments in my life where I've felt powerful, but this feels different. It feels more grounded within me and somehow more permanent, where in the past, I'd have flitted in and out of this wondrous state of being.

What does it mean to stand in your power?

To me, a person in their power is someone who's thinking, feeling and 'being' in their highest possible vibration. This means:

> A person in their power is someone who's thinking, feeling and 'being' in their highest possible vibration.

- They're tapping into the wisdom they've gained throughout their life to make conscious choices for their highest good.
- They're strongly connected to their intuition.
- They recognise themselves as a divine being.
- They take full responsibility for their life and their choices.
- Their shadows and their light are in balance.
- They're aware, open and grounded.

In short, their mind, body and soul are in complete alignment, and it's beautiful.

And what does that actually *feel* like?

The experience of standing in power will be different for each of us as we're all unique humans. For me, though, I feel it as brimming with energy, passion, creativity, inspired ideas, love and fire. I feel clear and emotionally balanced, and my vibration is at its peak.

In this state, I'm deeply connected to my intuition. I'm also strong and assertive, and I know my own mind and trust myself to make the right decisions for me.

I feel healthy, fit, super confident and deeply loving towards myself. On top of that, I'm motivated and focused, and I attract abundance into all areas of my life. And, finally, I'm open, aware and ready for new opportunities and learning.

> I've been fortunate to experience being fully in my power, and it is GLORIOUS.

Chapter 13: Reclaiming Your Power

I've been fortunate to experience being fully in my power, and it is GLORIOUS.

Sometimes, this state of being stays with me for just a little while. Other times, it stays longer. It comes when I follow my own teachings within this book.

But, because I'm a human being with a family, friends and career, I don't always manage this. Plus, of course, sometimes life throws things at me that make me falter on my own path and step onto another one for a while. And that's OK too because there's obviously something there I need to learn.

Being truly powerful requires constant learning and growth to keep evolving. Without that evolution, we become stagnant and stuck, which means we're no longer in our power.

That's why, when I realise I'm out of balance, I choose one or more of the exercises in this book to bring myself back onto my powerful path again. I ask myself questions to identify where I've stepped out of balance. Then, once the answer has been revealed, I get busy!

What it can feel like to be in your power

I believe that if you've followed and embodied all the teachings in this book, you should be feeling in your power right now. However, if you're not 100% sure, here are some signs to look for:

- You feel confident, strong, motivated and inspired, and your creativity is on fire.
- You consciously make positive choices for yourself, without doubting yourself or needing a second opinion.
- You're like a magnet for positive people and experiences, and you love them unconditionally.

- Everything in your life feels like it's flowing with ease, and you're attracting abundance in all areas of your life.
- You take amazing care of your mind, body and soul, so you're emotionally balanced, vibrant, energetic and strongly connected to your intuition.
- You use positive daily practices, such as a morning ritual and meditation.
- You're open to learning and new experiences.

Tips for stepping into your power

If you've never experienced being in your power before, or you feel like you've lost your way, here are a few tips to help you get on track:

- **Follow the five keys to wholistic living.** Remind yourself of them by re-reading Chapter 1 if you need to, and then use them to realign your energy.
- **Take stock of your life.** See where you can cut down on anything that causes you stress and depletes your energy. Ask yourself how you can live more in flow.
- **Don't spend time with people who diminish you.** Surround yourself with positive, inspiring people who are already vibing high. Energy is contagious!
- **Meditate on how you want to feel each day.** Then take action to bring those feelings to you. Want to feel physically super-strong? Get to the gym and lift some weights! Want to feel light and vibrant? Eat foods that are nourishing and give you a boost of energy. Want to feel relaxed? Allow yourself some rest!
- **Strengthen your intuition.** Try choosing an oracle or Tarot card every day for guidance as you learnt to do in Chapter 6.
- **Allow yourself to fully feel into every choice you need to make before you make it.** Does it feel light and good or heavy and hard? Always go with light and good!

Chapter 13: Reclaiming Your Power

- **Work with a mentor.** Again, sometimes you can only go so far on your own. Never be afraid to ask for help!

Something I recommend to everyone is setting your intentions before you even get out of bed in the morning and then writing up a daily schedule. This might sound boring to some people (not me – I freakin' love my lists!) Seriously, though, the best way to achieve your goals is to set them out and then action them.

> Something I recommend to everyone is setting your intentions before you even get out of bed in the morning.

I have a daily intention book where I first list my three most important tasks for the day. Then I divide all my other tasks into categories, for example:

- business
- personal
- nourishment/movement
- spiritual
- house.

I also write down the feelings I want to experience each day and what food I'll eat.

This may sound like a lot, but it helps me to stay focused and on task to complete my goals. If I don't set my intentions each day, I easily get distracted by pretty, shiny things and people!

Your ritual work: powerful goddess

Intention

To reclaim your power in all areas of your life, including:

- being confidently assertive when you need to
- bringing positive energy to your relationships

- connecting deeply with your magick
- embracing your sexuality
- shining in your work or business
- stepping into success
- standing up for justice.

Timing

Waxing to Full Moon.

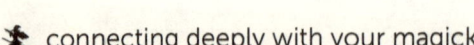

You will need

- A symbol of power: for example, you could use a crystal or piece of jewellery. I generally use my pentagram pendant. Or you could draw the symbol for power (find this on Google) on a piece of paper.
- A black pen.
- A piece of black paper.
- A piece of red paper.
- A cauldron or other heat-proof container.
- A crystal that represents power to you. I like black obsidian, black tourmaline, tiger's eye or garnet.
- A black candle.
- A red candle.
- Powdered incense: use any that resonates with you or make this power blend I created (either a pinch of each or whatever feels right to you):
  - cinnamon
  - chrysanthemum
  - mugwort OR myrrh
  - dragon's blood resin
  - a few drops of jasmine essential oil
- A charcoal disc to burn the incense on.

Chapter 13: Reclaiming Your Power

- 🜨 Some earth or sand in a heat-proof container for the charcoal disc.
- 🜨 Rose petals: fresh is great, but you can also use dried.

Ritual steps

1. Set up your altar space in a private place where you won't be disturbed
2. Cleanse your space and the tools/supplies you'll use, then have a cleansing bath or shower by candlelight, chanting the goddess Lilith's name.
3. Sit before your altar, and light the black candle and incense. Make sure to place the charcoal disc on either sand or earth in the heat-proof container.
4. On the black paper, write down the ways in which you've given away your power.
5. Set the paper alight and drop it into the cauldron or heat-proof container.
6. Carve the word 'Power' into the red candle, then light it.
7. On the red paper, write down the ways in which you invite your power back into you. Place the paper on your altar (anywhere that feels good) and then visualise yourself standing anew in your power and glory.
8. Speak the following chant into the crystal:

> "Lilith, I ask you to stand witness unto me.
> As I reclaim my power, to become all I can be.
> Shackles begone, I now stand free.
> To reclaim what's mine, my power is divine.
> By the power of three times three, this
> is my will, and so it shall be."

9. Pass your crystal through the incense smoke, and place it in front of the candle with your symbol and red paper. Sprinkle it with rose petals, and leave the candle to burn out.
10. From the next morning, wear your crystal on you to remind yourself daily of your power.

Integrating these teachings into your wholistic lifestyle

Start by asking yourself the questions in the journalling tasks on the following page. Then:

- **Again, check in with the five keys to wholistic living.** Are you living in alignment with them? If not, note where you need to give more energy and begin doing what you need to do.
- **Make sure you use a morning ritual to start your day with intention.** For example, every morning, I sit before my altar and light a candle for focus. Then I cleanse myself with a smudge stick and breathe myself into stillness for a few minutes. Finally, I connect with the Goddess and God, express my gratitude to the Universe, and choose an oracle card for guidance.
- **Check how your thoughts are right now.** Are they positive and nurturing, or is there some negative self-talk going on? Thoughts are powerful, and when they're more positive, you're more likely to reach your goals. So make sure they're in order!
- **Do some of the healing techniques shared in this book.** Alternatively, work with a mentor to unlock any blocks that are still preventing you from stepping into your power.

Book of Shadows

☽ You might like to record your ritual and the power ceremony.

Chapter 13: Reclaiming Your Power

Journal tasks

Journal the following:

- What does a powerful person look like to you?
- Where have you given away your power in the past?
- Who do you admire as a powerful person and what attributes do you think make them powerful? For example:
  - I really admire Cate Blanchett for her beauty and integrity.
  - I admire my mother for her strength and dedication to doing what has to be done, as well as her adventurous spirit.
  - I admire Kat Von D for her dedication to her lifestyle and her business.

  My recognition of these women — and many more — for how they stand in their power inspires me to strengthen these attributes within myself.

- What powerful attributes would you like to nurture within yourself?
- What does it feel like when you're in your power? If you haven't experienced this feeling yet, what do you think it would feel like?
- If you're not quite there yet, what do you need to nurture in your life to reach the point of fully stepping into your power?
- Make an action plan.

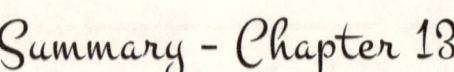

Summary – Chapter 13

- 🧙 I don't believe it's possible to stay in your power 100% of the time, because you're constantly learning, integrating and growing.
- 🧙 You can, however, step *back* into your power at any time by using the advice in this chapter.
- 🧙 Standing in your power can look different for everyone, and the first step in reclaiming your own power is to identify how that looks and feels for you.
- 🧙 Stepping into your power brings you the strength and confidence to live as you choose and bring your dreams to reality.
- 🧙 Before you can step into your power, it's important to identify where you've been giving it away and work to change your behaviour around that.
- 🧙 The best practical way to begin the journey to reclaiming your power is to follow the five keys to wholistic living, which will realign your energy.

Conclusion

Our time together is drawing to a close...

I dearly hope you've enjoyed this book and that it's taken you on a magickal journey.

I'd like you to take a moment here to remember where you began and to tune in to how different you feel now from when you first started. I'm guessing that when you were drawn to pick up this book, it was because you were looking for something. Or perhaps you'd just stepped onto your magickal path and were keen for guidance?

Regardless of whatever drew you here and inspired you to read, I hope you have experienced a journey of discovery, learning, healing and growth.

In the beginning, you learnt about the foundations of a wholistic lifestyle and how this impacts your craft. You discovered why it's important to understand how the natural world works, as well as how to connect with the Divine (and therefore, the Divine within yourself).

From there, you went on to discover the tools you'll need to move forward positively and with strength on your journey. You learnt how to read signs and how to create sacred spaces to work and live in. And – perhaps most importantly – you learnt how to be intentional about who you include in your circle to support you. These are all essential to successfully empower yourself.

Lastly, the final section asked you to dig deep to really connect with the truth of who you are. You learnt healing techniques that are designed to both aid you in your daily life and equip you for your shadow journeys. And you learnt that shadow work can help you to shed what you no longer need, so you can finally step into your truth – and, ultimately, your power.

Everything you've read about is something I've experienced myself. Over many, many years, those experiences have brought me to a place where I love myself and my life – even when it's challenging.

So I truly believe that, whether you've just dipped your toes in for now or you've taken an entire journey, you'll experience positive shifts. And those positive effects will continue to ripple out into your life.

But the next part of your journey is just beginning

While this journey with me is almost at an end, it's far from the end for you. Everything you've learnt has prepared you to embark on the next phase of your life. As long as you're here on this physical Earth plane, you'll continue to evolve and grow – so I urge you to continue with the practices you've learnt here.

For example, I've taken many shadow journeys now, and each one looks and feels completely different. In each one, I continue to peel back layers of myself to reveal new things I need to heal.

Just as I have, you'll be able to apply many of the techniques in this book to new journeys, new healings and new rituals.

Conclusion

Your final ritual work: the completion ceremony

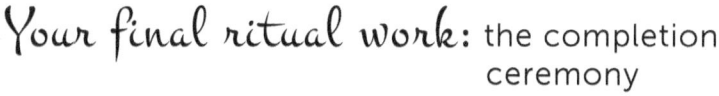

Below is one last ceremony for this book to celebrate everything you've achieved and all the ways in which you've grown and evolved on your journey. I'd recommend performing it once you've completed all the reading and practical actions within this book.

If you've already done that, congratulations on your journey! I trust that if you've followed my advice and done all the practical tasks, you're feeling pretty magickal right now!

Please note: it's quite symbolic to step through a doorway of some sort – perhaps a garden arch or the space between two perfectly aligned trees – as part of this ritual. This acts almost as a portal, taking you from one dimension or energy state to another.

Intention

To mark the completion of this part of your journey into a life of wholistic witchcraft.

Timing

Once you've completed your journey through this book.

You will need

- A crown of some sort. This can be a simple one made out of flowers or greenery, for example.
- A red candle.
- A lighter or matches.
- The crystal from your power ritual in Chapter 13.
- Salt for your cleansing shower.

- Two heat-proof bowls, plus sand or earth, and a charcoal disc. I recommend breaking the charcoal disc in half and using one half for each bowl.
- Leftover incense from your power ritual, or dried sage.

Ritual steps

1. Prepare everything you'll need for your ceremony. Have your crystal and red candle on one side of the arch/tree portal, and the incense burners/heat-proof bowls set up inside each side of the arch/portal.

    Place your crown on the opposite side of the arch/portal.

2. Prepare yourself as you usually would for a ritual by having a cleansing shower and scrubbing your body with the salt mixed with a little water.

3. Dress in something that makes you feel magickal.

4. Light the charcoal discs and sprinkle both with incense. Use a good pinch on each, so that it burns for a while.

5. Sit before the red candle, light it and focus on the flame to help connect with your intention.

    Meditate for a few moments on the journey you've just completed. Think about the highs, the lows, the lessons, the a-ha moments and how you feel now compared to how you felt when you started.

6. Stand up, holding onto your empowered crystal. Walk through the incense smoke and through the arch/portal.

    Feel the energy of leaving the old version of yourself behind as you step into the new you. When you're on the other side, pick up your crown and place it on your head.

7. Spend a moment celebrating all that you've been, all that you are and all that you've yet to become.

8. Walk forth into your new life as the powerful person you've now become.

Conclusion

Note: You might like to do something after this ceremony to continue celebrating the completion of your journey. Perhaps you could have dinner with friends or buy yourself something symbolic to mark this special occasion.

Where you go next is up to you

As you continue to grow, you'll inevitably go deeper within yourself. At times, you may feel like you need some additional support.

I'd encourage you here again to seek out like-minded people – maybe through local groups or circles. You could even start a book club to work through this book, either in person or online!

As I've mentioned frequently, a mentor can often help to push you further than you've been able to go yourself. However, it's important to find the right one to support your journey. If you don't already know where to find one, you could search online in your local area or ask for recommendations.

If you've enjoyed working through this book with me and have resonated with what I've shared, you might like to take it further by connecting with me in person or online. I offer many circles and workshops, personal mentoring and online rituals/courses that support you to keep moving forward and growing.

You'll find more about all of my offerings and how to stay in touch on the next page. In the meantime, it's my heartfelt wish that you've loved the wisdom you've gained here enough to now take it and run with it.

May your days and your life be filled with so much love, inspiration, healing, growth and – of course – magick.

Blessings to you,

Bella x

Yearning to Go Deeper?

If you'd like to explore the realms of magick, healing or wholistic living further, you can connect with me in many ways, both in person or online.

In-person options

My studio in Buderim, QLD, Australia offers a range of wholistic beauty treatments, magickal mentoring and intuitive Tarot readings.

In this sacred space, I also run regular circles for maidens, mothers and goddesses, along with workshops to propel you forward on your magickal journey.

I also run magickal *Witches and Wildlings* weekend retreats twice yearly on the Sunshine Coast. These are a deep immersion into magick, ritual and wholistic health. Information about upcoming retreats is available on my website.

Online options

At my website www.wiccid.com.au, you'll find all my products, tickets to events and access to my Academy of Witchcraft & Magick. This includes my 12-month Apprenticeship program, which takes you through a journey from beginner witchling to proficient sorcerer level.

Wholistic Witchcraft

The Apprenticeship includes:

- lessons that you can read online or print
- downloadable meditations
- online support via the website learning portal and a Facebook group
- the opportunity to attend live workshops and circles.

    Find out more at https://wiccid.com.au/wiccid-academy-of-witchcraft-magick/.

Magickal tools and products

Finally, I produce a range of magickal products that are designed to enhance and aid your magickal journey. These include:

- ritual kits
- incenses
- cleansing sprays
- potions
- meditation CDs.

These are all available through my online store: www.wiccid.com.au/shop.

Other ways to stay in touch

To find out more about any of my offerings, please head to my website. Or, to ask about booking an appointment, email me at bella@wiccid.com.au

If you'd like to connect with me on social media, you can find me:

- on Facebook at www.facebook.com/WiccidHolisticTherapies
- on Instagram at www.instagram.com/wiccidholistictherapies.

Yearning to Go Deeper?

Or, finally, join my mailing list for a monthly dose of magickal inspiration at www.wiccid.com.au/wiccidmagickmail.

What's it like to work with Belinda?

Barbara: Academy of Witchcraft and Magick

"I've been a participant in Bella's Wiccid Academy for over a year, and I highly recommend it! Bella loves what she does, and this comes through in her warmth, her insight and the great circles and workshops she provides for all her members. It's been a wonderful learning experience, and I look forward to learning more this year!"

Jennifer: Healing session

"Holy hell, Mother of God! I went into a session expecting a gentle ThetaHealing, but it turned out that the Divine had other ideas. Words cannot describe the level of integration I experienced on Bella's table. It was an extremely profound – yet emotionally gentle and enjoyable – session. Massive shifts.

"I've been receiving energy healings and transmissions for years, but what happened today was exactly what my body and soul has been waiting for. So much gratitude to you, girlfriend!"

Emily: Everything!

"I cannot recommend Bella and Wiccid enough. She's been such a blessing in my life for so many reasons. Whether Bella's doing my nails or creating my incenses, or I'm attending her retreats, partaking in her rituals and going to her circles, the amount of love, time, effort and QUALITY she puts into every service she offers speaks for itself.

"She's helped me to transform my life in so many ways, and I know if you're reading this that she can do the same for you too."

Melissa: Wiccid Witches & Wildlings Retreat

"I returned from a Wiccid retreat with Bella with a feeling of lightness, joy and purpose. I've been trying to achieve this on my own and now know that I wouldn't have got there without Bella. She had an amazingly relaxing, supportive way of taking us through the shadow work and bringing us out the other end reborn.

"I couldn't have asked for a better group of ladies to do this with. We all walked in as strangers and instantly became friends. Thank you, all – and of course, mostly Bella and her wonderful team of helpers."

Pammy: Everything

"I've been blessed to have had many sessions with Bella, from beauty therapies to healing therapies. A massage from Bella is more than a massage – it's aetheric healing as well.

"I was also fortunate enough to win a 12-month Apprenticeship with the Academy of Witchcraft and Magick. I eagerly looked out for each month's PDF training, which had so much information and tasks to do. I loved it, and even now refer to it when I'm seeking information. Love you, Bella!"

Janette: Healing

"I'm so glad I found Bella – she's amazing. I felt pretty broken at first, but working with Bella has given me back my direction. We did a few different things and each week I did my homework; Bella was always at hand to help if I wandered off track. Thank you, Bella, for helping me to help myself."

Adele: Circles

"Since my daughters started Magickal Maidens and I now attend Bella's various beautiful circles, I can honestly say that my girls and I are closer for it. These circles are done from a pure place and an open heart. We're so much happier for going, and we feel like we were always supposed to be here."

Yearning to Go Deeper?

Karen: Workshops

"I've attended several workshops with Bella now, and I've really enjoyed each one. I've learnt loads and met some really lovely people. If you want to get into witchcraft or just creating in a comfortable space with non-judgemental, fun, like-minded people, Wiccid is definitely the go-to. Thank you so much, Bella!"

Ren: Academy of Witchcraft and Magick

"The Wiccid Academy has changed my life. This course, run by the vivacious Goddess Bella, has helped to change my thinking, manifest new ideas and create beautiful rituals to better my life and the lives of those around me.

"The time and intricate detail Bella puts into each month's lessons is simply magickal! She provides each student with regular mentoring sessions, and I found this really helped me to feel connected and learn so much more.

"Bella is highly knowledgeable in so many different areas, and I highly recommend this course to anyone and everyone interested in bettering their Inner Goddess.

Blessed be ♥.

Tina: Academy of Witchcraft and Magick

"Bella has created an extremely comprehensive course that gives a very good understanding of working with magickal energies to enhance your life. She even puts together beautiful magickal boxes to purchase containing the tools for each workbook if you need them."

Laura: Academy of Witchcraft and Magick – Lilith Ritual

"I found this course game-changing. Easy-to-follow daily challenges and rituals helped me to align my Self and soul, and really dig into personal issues to move forward with positive growth. Bella gave so much support and love throughout – xx."

Acknowledgements

Thank you to my husband Adrian for your love and support throughout the process of writing this book. I couldn't have done it without you.

Thank you to my daughters, Tori and Aynslie, for loving me, supporting me in writing this book, keeping things real and making me laugh when I needed it.

Thank you to Mum and Dad. You are my world and my rocks. Your support throughout my life and – in particular – for my business means everything.

Thank you to my sister-friend Tina for reaching out to me years ago. Thank you for inviting me to the fateful meeting that ultimately helped me step right out of the broom closet. Your love, friendship and ongoing support are constant sources of light in my life, and this book wouldn't have been created without you.

Thank you to my sister-friend Nicole for being my constant muse. Thank you for loving me through thick and thin, and for always being on hand with truth and advice when I've needed it.

Thank you to my sacred inner circle of friends – you know who you are. Each one of you has supported me, believed in me and encouraged me from Day 1, and I appreciate you more than I can say.

Thank you to each and every client who's ever connected with me, whether through my wholistic practice, my circles or my Academy. So many of you have become dear sisters and friends. I appreciate the love and light you bring to my life every day.

Wholistic Witchcraft

Thank you to Catherine for creating the illustrations for the witchling's journey at the beginning of each section. You really got inside my head and brought the witchling to life – I love her so much!

Finally, thank you to Alex, my editor Tanja, and everyone else involved in bringing this book to life. I've deeply appreciated your professionalism, honesty, integrity and support.

APPENDIX A

Sabbats

The Wheel of the Year – the sabbats

There are eight sabbats that are celebrated by most Witches, Wiccans and other Pagans throughout the year. These eight sacred days make up the Wheel of the Year, and each one marks an important turning point in Nature's annual cycles.

Following the Wheel of the Year allows us to live more in tune with Nature and each season's natural rhythms. This, in turn, means we can move with the natural energies to give our magick more power and our daily lives more flow.

The Wheel is made up of two groups of four holidays, as shown in the tables below. Note that for the solar festivals, solstices are the dates of the longest day or night. Equinoxes are the dates when the day and night are of exactly the same length.

The Greater Sabbats: solar festivals			
Sabbat	Time of solar year	Southern Hemisphere date	Northern Hemisphere date
Ostara	Spring Equinox	September 20–21	March 20–21
Midsummer/Litha	Summer Solstice	December 21–22	June 20–21
Mabon	Autumn Equinox	March 20–21	September 20–21
Yule	Winter Solstice	June 20–21	December 21–22

The Lesser Sabbats: fire festivals		
Sabbat	Southern Hemisphere date	Northern Hemisphere date
Beltane	October 31–November 1	April 30–May 1
Lughnasadh	February 1	August 1
Samhain	April 30–May 1	October 31–November 1
Imbolc	August 1	February 1

As each sabbat follows Nature's cycles, each one has different associations, such as crystals, colours, gods/goddesses, herbs and incenses.

I encourage you to do further research on the sabbats if learning more interests you. See my recommended reading list in Appendix I for my favourite book on sabbats.

Foods sacred to the sabbats

These are handy for offerings and feasts.

- **Ostara:** asparagus, cupcakes, dill, eggs, fruits, grains, green vegetables, honey, lamb, lettuce, radishes, seafood, sesame or sunflower seeds, spring onions.
- **Litha:** cheese, fresh fruits, honey, pine nuts, pumpernickel bread, semi-dried tomatoes, spinach, squash, sunflower seeds.
- **Mabon:** barley, bread, gourds, grapes, harvest fruits and vegetables, nuts, oats, rye, seeds, wheat.
- **Yule:** baked goods, caraway seed rolls, casseroles, citrus fruits, dried fruit and nuts, fruit cake, pork dishes, roast meats, root vegetables, seeds, turkey.

Appendix A: Sabbats

- **Yule drinks:** coffee and hot chocolate, eggnog, hot buttered rum, hot toddy (lemon, honey, alcohol and boiled water), mulled wine, tea.
- **Beltane:** almonds, honey, light cakes, marigold custard, mushrooms, oatcakes, radish, vanilla ice cream.
- **Lughnasadh:** berry pies, breads, elderberry wine and mead, fresh fruits, oatcakes, seeds and grains, starchy vegetables such as corn and potatoes.
- **Samhain:** apples, beetroot, blueberries and blackberries, corn, fermented foods, meat – especially pork, nuts, pomegranates, pears, pineapple, pumpkin and pumpkin dishes such as pumpkin pie, squash, strawberries, turnips.
- **Imbolc:** bannocks (scone-like bread), cakes and pancakes, cheese, dried fruit, dried or salted meats, eggs, grains, nuts, potatoes, pickled foods, polenta/cornmeal.

APPENDIX B

Colours

You can use colour in both your rituals and daily life to change energy, help you focus or create a feeling. Using colour magick can be as simple as wearing certain coloured clothing or placing a coloured cloth on your altar to *bring in* the energy of that colour.

For example:

- If I wanted to feel powerful, I might wear red.
- If I wanted to do a healing spell, I might use a blue cloth on my altar.
- If I wanted to bring more love energy into my home, I might buy some pink flowers.
- If I wanted to stimulate one of my chakras, I might breathe in that colour during a meditation.

See below for correspondences to the various colours and allow your intuition to guide you.

White

White represents the Goddess, the ancient mother, and devotion to the Divine and the feminine mysteries. It's also the colour of the crown chakra.

Use white for clarity, decreasing anxiety, forgiveness, freedom, goodwill, health, illumination, initiation, liberation, love, neatness and cleanliness, new beginnings, perfection, protection, purity and purification, simplicity, spirituality and unity.

Black

Black is the colour of the Dark Goddess, and of winter, chaos and the mysteries. It absorbs all colours and – if you use a black and white candle together – it can bring balance.

Use black to dispel negativity or return it to the sender, and to help you deal with emotional stress and trauma. Use it also as a veil to cloak what you don't wish others to see. Finally, use it for banishing, divination, hibernation, keeping secrets, New Moon ceremonies, protection, rebirth, rest, shadow work and wisdom.

Grey

Grey is the colour of neutrality, stability and the ability to be unemotional. Use it to calm someone with a tendency to be impulsive or to help you accept change.

Also use grey for acceptance, composure, dignity, endurance, glamour magick and respect, or for patience when you're waiting to gather details for a situation. Team grey with green when you're applying for a loan or asking for a pay increase.

Silver

Silver is associated with the Moon, so use it for Moon magick – especially for harnessing the intuitive powers of the Moon. For the same reason, use it when doing the Charge of the Goddess or for any other feminine magick. Additionally, this colour can help lovers open their hearts and help you to open yourself to the possibility of love.

Silver is also associated with money and bringing in money quickly, and can also help with releasing and cleansing negative energy. Psychically, use silver for astral travel, dreams and visions, personal illumination and revealing your potential.

Appendix B: Colours

Other associations include seeing through illusions, as well as emotions, endurance, fluidity, freedom, meditation, mystery, peace, reality, restoring balance and tidal magick.

Gold

Gold is associated with the Sun and sun gods like Apollo.

Use it for connecting with your higher Self, as well as increasing confidence, optimism and positivity. Alternatively, use it to bring money and material wealth, prosperity and abundance, and recognition and success.

Other associations include achievement and triumph of all kinds, ambition, attraction, extravagance, health, healing, magick and warmth.

Red

Red is associated with masculine energy, summer and the root chakra. Use it to stop something or for banishing spells that involve fire.

Red is the colour of blood, Earth energy, grounding, safety and stability. Yet, at the same time, it's also the colour of anger and rage, determination, fire, passion, power, and sexual energy and lust.

Use red for action, confidence, courage, energy, expansion, leadership, life force, motivation, renewal of life, strength and survival.

Orange

Orange is associated with the sacral chakra and with abundance, fertility, material gain and success. Use it for overcoming challenges, removing blocks and bringing projects to fruition.

Emotionally, orange is the colour of joy and happiness. It brings a positive outlook, helping you to recover from grief and despair, and uplifting and revitalising you. Use it to help release abandonment issues, bring warmth to your relationship and help you to communicate in social situations.

Other associations include acceptance, attraction, comfort, creativity, health, motivation, opportunity, pleasure, self-esteem, sexuality and feeling or offering welcome.

Yellow

Yellow is also associated with the Sun and the solar plexus chakra.

It's the colour of balance, business smarts, intellect, learning and intellectual achievement, and the mind. Other associations include blessings (particularly of the home), goodness and safe travel.

Use yellow for beauty, communication and expression, contacting your spirit guides, detecting and dealing with treachery, happiness, healing, humility, intuition, joy and fun, light, prosperity, self-esteem, trust and truth.

Green

Green is the colour of Mother Earth, the Green Man and spring. This means it's associated with balance, gardening, growth, Nature and Nature magick.

It's also the colour of the heart chakra and of Venus. In this realm, it's associated with attraction, emotions, love – especially new love and unconditional, universal love – and harmony between the head and heart.

Other associations include abundance and prosperity, deciphering right from wrong, happiness, healing, hope and promise, money, new

Appendix B: Colours

beginnings, positivity, renewal and rebirth, peace-making, tranquillity and youth.

Wear green when you need help with something.

Blue

Blue is the colour of Vishnu, Jupiter and Atlantis. It's also the colour of the throat chakra and of clear communication.

Use blue when you're dealing with officials or to protect your reputation or defeat an enemy. Alternatively, use it to help build lasting relationships.

Other associations include authenticity, calm and tranquillity, clarity, cleansing, faith, healing, intelligence, justice, limitless possibilities, loyalty, meditation, peace, protection, trust, truth and wisdom.

Indigo

Indigo is associated with the third eye chakra, intuition and connecting with the cosmos.

Use it in meditation to go deeper, or for tapping into your psychic and telepathic abilities.

Other associations include midnight magick, higher consciousness and wisdom.

Purple

Purple is the colour of royalty and is worn by deities, kings and queens. It's sacred to Osiris and also relates to Jupiter.

It's the colour of the crown chakra, spirituality, spiritual awareness and the higher Self. Psychically, it's associated with clairvoyance, connecting with the ancient ones, gaining the 'sight' or other psychic abilities, magick, mystery, receiving divine wisdom, trusting your inner voice and understanding dreams.

More mundane associations include dealings with the government, finding your life purpose, forgiveness, intelligence, justice and truth.

Pink

Pink is the colour of Venus and the heart chakra. In this realm, it's associated with affection, compassion, harmony, love – especially self-love and unconditional, universal love – and romance.

Other associations include comfort, femininity, friendship, gentleness, healing – both emotionally and generally, peace, reconciliation and resolving conflict, softness and warmth.

Use pink in blessings for a baby girl.

Brown

Brown is the colour of Earth, life, Nature magick, root power and affinity with the natural world.

Use it to connect with ancestors and access instinctive wisdom. You can also wear it to avoid being misled.

Other associations include emotional soothing, friendship, honesty, loyalty, grounding, practicality, protection, regeneration, security, support, transformation and trustworthiness.

APPENDIX C

Crystals

The power of crystal energy can enhance your daily life and your magick. Use them in your rituals, keep them in the rooms of your home or close by you, or wear them on you.

Please note: I've mentioned earlier in the book that I've taken crystal remedies. DO NOT make your own unless you're an experienced practitioner as some crystals are toxic when taken internally.

Agate

Connection to Earth energy, courage, emotional balance, grounding, harmony, healing, love, peace, protection, stability, strength, support, throat chakra.

Types: blue lace agate, dendritic agate, fire agate, moss agate.

Amber

Anxiety relief, attraction – especially of lasting love, beauty, clearing the mind, digestion, dissolving negativity, drawing off toxins, eliminating fears, fertility, headache relief, healing pain and disease, helping with impotence, increasing radiance and vitality, love, luck, patience, protection, purifying, sacral chakra, strength, wisdom.

Amber is also good for empaths as it wards off negative energy from others.

Amethyst

Creativity, crown chakra, dreams (including curing nightmares), happiness, healing, love, luck, overcoming alcoholism, peace, prosperity, protection – especially against psychic attack, psychic powers, sleep, soothing emotions, stimulating your mind.

Amethyst also helps to keep bad habits in check.

Types: ametrine, chevron amethyst, rutilated amethyst.

Aventurine

Eyesight, healing, heart chakra, luck, manifesting, mental powers, money, opportunity, optimism, peace, releasing old patterns, soothing anger, stimulating physical growth, winning.

Aventurine can guard against smog, pollution and geopathic stress.

Bloodstone

Balancing masculine and feminine energies, banishing evil and negativity, base chakra, calming the mind, clarity, cleansing, courage and strength, creativity, dreams, gardening, grounding, healing, intuition, nurturing, prosperity, protection, reducing anger, revitalising, stimulating metabolism and immunity, stimulating success, wealth.

Carnelian

Accelerating healing, balancing energy, banishing apathy, breaking bad habits, communication, courage, creativity, determination, endurance, fertility, healing arthritis and lower back pain, joy, love, motivation, peace, positivity, prosperity and good luck, protection – especially of the home, sacral chakra, stabilising, success.

Appendix C: Crystals

Carnelian can help to overcome the trauma of abuse and help you to make positive choices for yourself.

Types: orange, pink orange, red, scarlet.

Citrine

Alignment, alleviating nightmares, attraction, cleansing and regenerating, comfort, concentration, confidence, creativity, detoxifying the blood, digestion, easing depression, easing fears and phobias, emotional balance, enthusiasm, fast money, motivation, prosperity, protection, psychic powers, releasing negative qualities, removing cellulite, self-expression, solar plexus chakra, spiritual growth, stabilising, success, truth.

Types: various shades of pale yellow to deep orange.

Coral

Base chakra, calming emotions, community, connecting with ocean energy, friendship, gardening, healing – especially for bones, heightening intuition and opening imagination, honesty, optimism, passion, peace, positivity, protection – especially when travelling over water, regulating menstruation, releasing unhealthy thoughts, strengthening visualisation skills, transformation, wisdom.

Types: black, blue, brown, red.

Fluorite

Balancing energy, calming, cleansing, concentration, creativity, discovering your divine purpose, healing, improving balance – both mentally and physically, making decisions, mending your aura, mental strength and clarity, neutralising negative energy, past-life peace, positivity, regression, soothing emotions, technology, third eye chakra.

Types: blue, green, rainbow, yellow.

Hematite

Absorbing negative energy, alleviating worry and stress, anchoring to Earth, balancing and centring, blood purifying, calming, clearing anxiety, confidence, cooperation, divination, energising, focusing, grounding, healing, helping the ascension process, manifesting, protection, seeing the positive side of things.

Jade

Circulation, dreams, emotional healing, friendship, gardening, going deep spiritually, good luck, harmony, healing – especially for the liver and kidneys, heart chakra, love, meditation, money and wealth, prosperity, protection, releasing negative thoughts and patterns, soothing and calming skin, stabilising, vitality and longevity, wisdom.

Types: black, blue, brown, lavender, orange, red, purple, white, yellow.

Jasper

Aligning the chakras, courage, grounding and centring, healing – excellent for recuperation, heart chakra, fertility, improving relationships, increasing physical energy, justice, nurturing, protection – particularly from physical harm and when travelling, raising vibration, restful sleep, stability, strength, tranquillity, warmth, wisdom.

Jasper may also help to treat disorders of the kidney, spleen and liver.

Types: brown, bumblebee, green, leopard, ocean, picture, red, yellow.

Appendix C: Crystals

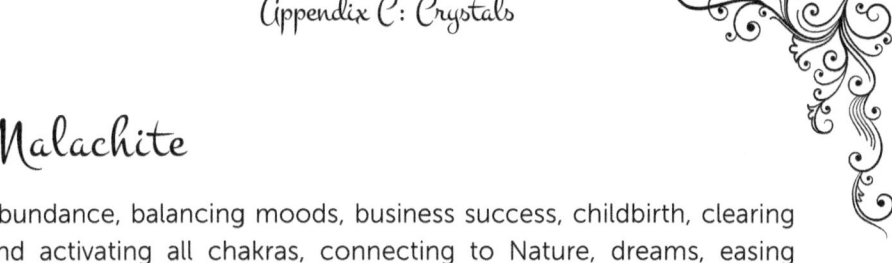

Malachite

Abundance, balancing moods, business success, childbirth, clearing and activating all chakras, connecting to Nature, dreams, easing menstrual cramps, empathy, energy clearing, expression, fresh starts, healing, heart chakra, love, lowering blood pressure, opening, peace, personal growth, power, protection, removing blockages, removing pollution, resolving abuse trauma, tapping into warrior energy, transformation.

Moonstone

Balancing women's cycles, boosting business, calming, connecting to the Divine Feminine, crown chakra, digestion, divination, easing stress, gardening, good luck, growth, inspiration, intuition, love, Moon magick, new beginnings, patience, protection, psychic powers, reflecting, releasing fluid retention, sleep, soothing emotional imbalances, strength, success, youth.

Types: blue, brown, green, grey, rainbow, white, yellow.

Obsidian

Absorbing negative environmental energies, clearing emotional baggage, divination, grounding, growth, healing, peace, prophecy, protection, psychic cleansing, relieving stress, scrying, self-reflection, shadow work, shielding against negativity, spiritual communication, truth.

Obsidian can also help to release anger, fear, resentment and toxic people.

Types: black, blue, brown, green, purple, rainbow, snowflake.

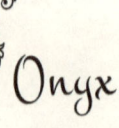

Onyx

Absorbing negativity, base chakra, confidence, defensive magick, facing fears, grounding, inner work and shadow journeys, meditation, opening chakras, physical strength and stamina, protection, public speaking, releasing/letting go – especially of negative thoughts, support during grieving.

Types: black, brown, colourless, green, pink, red.

Quartz (general)

Amplifying energy, clarity, cleansing, clearing and energising all chakras, clearing negativity, contacting those who've passed, crown chakra, expanding consciousness, growth, healing, lifting vibration, love, manifestation, meditation, power, prosperity, protecting your aura, psychic powers, soothing migraines, success, transformation, transmuting energy.

Types: blue, clear, rose, rutilated, smoky, snow.

Sodalite

Balancing metabolism, clairvoyance, communication, confidence, easing panic attacks, expressing feelings, healing, heart and throat chakras, inspiration, intuition, meditation, peace, positive self-esteem, positivity, rational thought, regaining composure, relieving throat issues, safe travel, self-trust, soothing disagreements, truth, wisdom, writing.

Sunstone

Abundance, alleviating stress, clearing and energising all chakras, commitment, dissolving fear, encouraging promotion, energy, healing for cancer, health, helping your authentic Self shine, independence, intuition, joy, leadership, light, luck, originality, positivity, protection, relieving depression, Sun energy, strength, vitality.

Tiger's eye

Alleviating anxiety, awareness, base chakra, business aid, confidence, courage, creativity, detoxifying, divination, emotional balance, energy, focus and mental clarity, growth, home harmony, insight, luck, money, powerful protection – especially from psychic attacks, quick thinking, reducing cravings, resolving problems, supporting you in putting yourself out there, truth.

Types: cat's eye (red), falcon's eye (blue), ox eye (brownish red).

APPENDIX D
Gods and Goddesses

Below are a few of the more well-known gods and goddesses that can help you with your magickal work when you call on them.

Reminder: please research the deities you want to work with *before* you call them in, and then make sure you connect with them respectfully.

- **Apollo**: Greek god of the Sun.
- **Artemis**: Greek goddess of the hunt.
- **Brigid**: Celtic goddess of spring, fertility, healing, poetry and smithcraft.
- **Cernunnos**: Celtic 'Horned God' of animals, fertility, life, wealth and the Underworld.
- **Cerridwen**: Celtic goddess of death and rebirth. She's also the patron of witches and is associated with fertility, the Moon, poetry, prophecy and science.
- **Changing Woman**: Navajo goddess of the Blessings Ceremonies, Earth, food, plants maturing and the seasons.
- **Demeter**: Greek goddess of the harvest, life and death, and sacred law.
- **Freyja**: Norse goddess of beauty, death, fertility, gold, love, sex, sorcery and war.
- **Ganesha**: Hindu god of the arts and sciences, intellect and wisdom, letters and learning during writing, as well as the parasu (axe), pasa (noose) and ankusa (elephant training hook).
- **Hades**: Greek god of the Underworld.

Wholistic Witchcraft

- 🜚 **Hecate:** Greek goddess of witchcraft, as well as the crossroads, magick and the night.
- 🜚 **Isis:** Egyptian fertility goddess. Also associated with magick, healing, motherhood and marriage.
- 🜚 **Kali:** Hindu goddess of creation, destruction, power and time. She's the one who bestows moksha (liberation) and is the destroyer of evil forces – a divine protector.
- 🜚 **Kokopelli:** Hopi god of agriculture, childbirth, fertility, music – especially the flute, and rain. He's also known as a 'trickster god' and is associated with animals that love water, such as snakes, lizards and insects.
- 🜚 **Kuan Yin:** Chinese goddess of compassion, as well as creativity, friendship, illusion, intelligence, magick and water. She's sometimes believed to be the mother of Gautama Buddha.
- 🜚 **Mars:** Roman god of war, destruction and masculinity. He's also the guardian of agriculture, farmers and soldiers.
- 🜚 **Neptune:** Roman god of fresh water and the sea, horses and horse racing, and the trident.
- 🜚 **Odin:** Norse 'All-Father' god of knowledge and wisdom. Also associated with battle, charms and magic, the gallows, healing, poetry, royalty, the runic alphabet, sorcery and the sabbat Yule.
- 🜚 **Osiris:** Egyptian god of life, death and rebirth. He was known as the 'Judge of the Dead' and presided over the cycles of Nature, regeneration, resurrection, transition and the Underworld.
- 🜚 **Oya:** Yoruba goddess of change, death and rebirth.
- 🜚 **Thor:** Norse god of thunder, as well as fertility, hallowing (making sacred), lightning, oak trees, protection of humanity, storms and strength.
- 🜚 **Uzume:** Japanese goddess of mirth and revelry, as well as the dawn, longevity, prosperity, protection and wisdom.

Appendix D: Gods and Goddesses

- **Venus:** Roman goddess of love. Her Greek counterpart is Aphrodite.
- **Zeus:** Greek god of the sky and thunder.

Representations of the Goddess

- cauldron
- cup
- five-petalled flowers
- mirror
- necklace
- seashell
- emerald
- pearl
- silver
- bat
- bee
- bear
- cat
- cow
- dog
- dolphin
- goose
- horse
- lion
- owl
- rabbit
- scorpion
- spider.

Representations of the God

- arrow
- brass
- candle
- diamond
- gold
- horns
- knife
- spear
- sword
- trident
- wand
- boar
- bull
- dog
- dragon
- eagle
- falcon
- fish
- lizard
- snake
- stag
- shark
- wolf.

APPENDIX E

Tools

Below is a handy, quick guide to some of the more common magickal tools and their uses. I've been collecting my tools for over 25 years from op shops, antique stores, online and local crafters of magickal things. I've also made a few tools of my own, such as one of my wands and my besom.

Take your time connecting with the tools meant for you, or design and craft your own.

- **Athame:** a magickal knife used to direct the energy you raise in your rituals. It's an instrument of command, power and energy manipulation.
- **Bell:** a tool to shift energy and clear it around your ritual space. You can also use it to signal a spell's beginning and end.
- **Besom:** a small magickal broom to 'sweep up' and clear negative or stagnant energies around your ritual space.
- **Boline:** a practical, working magickal knife. For example, you might use it to chop herbs for a spell or potion.
- **Cauldron:** a heat-proof container used for brewing, cooking and holding small fires.
- **Censer:** a vessel to hold your incense for ritual. It can be a special bowl or something special you find in Nature, such as a seashell.
- **Chalice:** a cup you use to hold water for the Water element on your altar or to hold the ritual beverage.
- **Wand:** a long, slender instrument of invocation that you can use to direct energy.

APPENDIX F

Animals

Some of us are blessed with animal familiars or have animal spirit guides who often visit us in dreams or visions. Other people regularly see animals in Nature that can be viewed as omens.

Regardless, you can utilise animal energies in your spellwork or to enhance your daily life. For example, many animals are sacred to particular gods and goddesses or sabbats. To call in a particular animal's energy, place a representation of it on your altar. Also be sure to look for omens from them, such as feathers.

Below I've listed just a few of the animals that I personally resonate and connect with. I encourage you to do further research of your own (see Appendix I).

- **Ant:** accomplishment, cooperation, determination, diligence, effort, industriousness, inspiration, patience, socialising, strength, teamwork.
- **Bat:** change, clairsentience, communication, family, fear, instinct, intuition, journeying, magick, the night, nurturing, rebirth, releasing, third eye chakra, transition, vision.
- **Bear:** authority, awakening the unconscious, balance, boundaries, confidence, courage, fearlessness, grounding, healing, hibernation, instinct, intuition, introspection, leadership, meditation, nurturing, power, resurrection, sleep, solitude, strength, vision quests.
- **Butterfly:** air, beauty, clarity, creativity, cycles, death, fertility, flowing through change, freedom, gentleness, growth, hibernation, joy, liberation, lightness, messages, movement,

omens, patience, potential, rebirth, releasing the old, silence, transformation.

- **Cat:** cleverness, the dark, discernment, divination, fruition of goals, independence, healing, intuition, magick, messages and communication, power, protection, resurrection and rebirth, sexual healing, weather prediction.

  Cats are also associated with a strong connection to the Goddess and the spirit world. They can act as a bridge between this world and the Otherworld.

- **Cow:** abundance, birth, calming, commitment, Divine Feminine, fertility, generosity, gentleness, grounding, healing, luck, Mother Earth, mothering, nourishment, patience, selflessness, strength.

- **Crow:** ancestors, change and transformation, death, destiny, divination, ethics, flexibility, instincts, integrity, intelligence, karma, law, luck, magick, mystery, prophetic insight, rebirth, spirit guides, spirituality, self-discovery, threefold law, transition, trickery and deception.

- **Deer:** abundance, action, adaptability, beauty, concealment, creativity, change, fertility, gentleness, grace, heart chakra, inner child connection, intuition, peace, regeneration, sensitivity, unconditional love.

- **Dog:** acceptance, adventure, bravery, communication, companionship, cooperation, devotion, energy and vitality, faith, fidelity, friendship, happiness, kindness, loyalty, patience, play, protection, reliability, tolerance, trust, unconditional love.

- **Dolphin:** balance, breath, community, curiosity, family, friendship, generosity, gentleness, grace, happiness, harmony, inner strength, intelligence, joy, nurturing, peace, play, power, protection, resurrection, sexuality.

- **Eagle:** courage, creativity, far-seeing, freedom, Great Spirit, healing, honesty and truth, hope, impatience, intuition, leadership, rebirth, resilience, sexual power stretching yourself, spring, vision.

Appendix F: Animals

Eagles are also known as the human connection to the Divine.

- **Frog:** abundance, adaptability, birth, cleansing, communication, connection to the Moon, dreaming, fertility, growth and transformation, healing, luck, opportunity, peace, purification, rain, releasing toxic emotions, self-care, spring, water, wisdom.

- **Horse:** ability, clairvoyance, endurance, faithfulness, fertility, freedom, friendship, guardianship, hard work, independence, intuition, movement, new directions and choices, nobility, overcoming obstacles, personal power, potential, pride, Spirit, stability, stamina, travel, trusting relationships, wisdom.

- **Lizard:** adaptability and going with the flow, balance, clairvoyance, cleansing negativity, detachment, dreaming, facing fear, healing, internal power, lucid dreaming, messages from the spirit world, movement, rebirth, regeneration, sensitivity, stillness, speed, spontaneity, the Sun.

  Lizards are also associated with helping to make you whole again after a rough time.

- **Moth:** air, allure, attraction, beauty, cleansing, death, determination, faith, growth, inner knowing, intuition, light, movement, optimism, passion, patience, psychic vision, secret knowledge, shadow work, transformation, vulnerability.

- **Owl:** change, clarity and clear vision, deception and the ability to see through it, details, discretion, femininity, freedom, intuition, magick, messenger, the Moon, movement, new beginnings, the night, omens, protection, removing illusion, secrets, shadow work, silence, transition, watchfulness, wisdom.

- **Possum:** adaptability, detecting or creating deception, diversion, diversity, defusing or causing drama, guidance, incubation, knowledge, mothering, opportunity, recovery, shape shifting, showing strength, strategy, talent.

- **Rabbit**: abundance, action, anxiety, awareness, cleverness, creativity, contradiction, cycles, family, fear, growth, harmony, instinct, luck, movement, Eostre/Ostara and spring, fertility, intuition, love, the Moon, opportunity, perception, rebirth, sensuality, speed, spontaneity, strength, timidity, work.

- **Rat**: abundance, adaptability, community, confidence, energy, fertility, foresight, humour, intelligence, intuition, inventiveness, letting go and moving on, movement, motivation, reproduction, resourcefulness, restlessness, shrewdness in business, stealth, strength, success, survival, wealth.

- **Snake**: adaptability, awareness, balance, change, (strong) connection to Mother Earth, creative life force, cunning, cycles, elusiveness, fertility, grief, grounding, healing, immortality, intuition, journeying, magick, moving forward, mysticism, patience, power, protection, rebirth, rejuvenation, release, transmutation, wisdom and knowledge.

- **Spider**: communication, construction, creativity, cycles, death, destiny, fear, feminine energy, growth, infinity, magick, mystery, networking, patience, protection, receptivity, reclaiming your power, renewal, resourcefulness, risk, shadow side, weaving, web of life, wisdom.

- **Turtle**: change, clarity, creation, determination, emotional strength, endurance, fertility, grounding, healing, knowledge, listening, longevity, the Moon, Mother Earth, order, patience, protection, stability, staying true to your path, survival, tranquillity, water, wisdom.

APPENDIX G

Herbs, Spices and Resins

Use herbs to bring a little magick into your cooking, natural beauty products, incenses, smudge sticks, charms and potions.

- **Allspice:** use to attract money and luck, as well as to heal acne, arthritis and digestion. Allspice can also increase circulation to your skin and freshen breath.
- **Basil:** use to bring balance to your mind, for love, happiness, peace, prosperity and protection. Basil will also prepare you for astral projection and other psychic journeys.
- **Bay leaf:** use to enhance your psychic abilities, for protection and getting rid of nasty spirits. For healing, use it to make a tea that will help to calm nerves, cleanse your body of impurities and aid digestion. Or make a poultice with the leaves and berries and place it on your chest to ease colds and flu.
- **Cinnamon:** use to raise your spiritual vibration and stimulate clairvoyance. It also draws love, happiness and prosperity, and will increase a male's passion. For healing, make a tea to stimulate your digestive system and relieve upset tummies.
- **Coriander:** use to attract fertility, good health, love and peace, and to enhance clairvoyance and divination skills. Coriander can also induce passion and invoke protection.
- **Dill:** use for love, luck, lust, money and protection. It will also bring inner understanding during vision quests. Place dill in a sachet and hang it over a baby's cot for protection, or use the sachet in a bath to make you irresistible to your lover.

Wholistic Witchcraft

- 🧙 **Lavender:** use for clarity, fertility, love, protection, purification, visions and wishes. It's also an aid for peace and sleep, and a treatment for headaches and digestion.

- 🧙 **Oregano:** use for happiness and joy, luck, protection, tranquillity, to bring visions and to deter troublemakers. Also use oregano in love spells, both to attract and to let go. For healing, it soothes digestion, nervous issues and coughs. Add to a bath to relax muscles, or drink in a tea to soothe a toothache.

- 🧙 **Parsley:** use for divination, fertility, good luck, happiness, health, lust and passion, protection, purification, strength and vitality. Also use to communicate with other realms and in rituals to honour those who've passed. For healing, use to treat urinary and kidney ailments. Make a compress to soothe swelling and puffiness.

- 🧙 **Rosemary:** use for attraction, intellect and memory, love, protection and purification. Also use it to deter thieves, dispel jealousy, encourage fidelity, and to remember past lives and dreams. Rosemary makes a wonderful hair tonic, can increase circulation and can also relieve aches and pains.

- 🧙 **Sage:** use for cleansing, granting wishes, healing, longevity and immortality, prosperity, protection and wisdom. Also use it to relieve grief and sadness, and to build courage and strength. For healing, use sage as a gargle for a sore throat or to boost insulin.

- 🧙 **Thyme:** use to enhance clairvoyance and cure nightmares, and for divination and protection. Also use it for courage, cleansing, consecration, happiness, healing, love, magick and money. For healing, use thyme as a cough remedy, or to aid digestion and deal with internal parasites.

Appendix G: Herbs, Spices and Resins

Resins

Resins start out as sap taken from injured trees, which solidifies and now carries powerful magickal properties. Use resins on their own or mix them with herbs and flowers to create specific incenses to burn on a charcoal disc.

- **Benzoin:** astral travel, blessings, business booster, clearing congestion, generosity, invoking visions, love magick, luck, mental powers, prosperity, purification, relieving depression, success.

- **Copal:** astral travel, banishing, cleansing, connection to the spiritual realm, crown chakra, happiness, inspiration, invocation, protection, purification, releasing anxiety and negative thoughts, spirituality, uplifting.

- **Dragon's blood:** banishing, cleansing, clearing negativity, courage, digestion, emotional strength, energy, exorcism, good luck, healing, increasing power in magickal workings, intention, love, manifestation, productivity, protection, sexual potency, strength.

- **Frankincense:** attraction, consecration, courage, exorcism, getting rid of negativity, good luck, healing and good health, joy, love, natural anti-depressant, protection, purification, safe travel, spirituality, strength, success, unblocking the sinuses.

    Also, use frankincense as an offering to sun gods.

- **Myrrh:** consecration, cleansing, clearing negative energy, connecting to the subconscious, divination, exorcism, healing, intuition, lifting vibration, meditation, peace, protection, purification, removing hexes, renewal, spiritual connection, third eye chakra.

APPENDIX H

Flowers

You can use flowers for all sorts of wonderful and magickal things, and bring their beautiful energy and healing properties into your daily life and rituals.

Simply keep a bunch of specific flowers in your home to benefit from their energies. Or, alternatively, add the petals, leaves and roots to incenses, healing poultices, smudge sticks and whatever else your mind can conjure!

Some of them can also be used in teas and cooking, but do your research: others can be toxic.

Here are just a few of my favourites and their associations:

- **Carnation**: balance, bringing stability to your love relationship, cleansing, creativity, energy, enhancing magickal powers, heart healing, optimism, perspective, protection, removing hexes, strength.
- **Chrysanthemum**: associated with the Sun, clarity, joy and happiness, protection – especially home protection, relieving insomnia, soothing for eyes and for grief, warding off evil spirits.
  Yellow chrysanthemum can help you find your voice.
- **Daffodil**: fertility, good luck, hope, love and self-love, mood enhancement, new beginnings, peace and calm, rebirth, renewal, spring magick, the Underworld.
  Wear a daffodil on you to bring good cheer.
  Warning: these flowers are toxic, so don't use them in cooking, healing medicine or in beauty remedies.

Wholistic Witchcraft

- **Dandelion:** sacred to Hecate:
  - Leaf – banishing negativity, healing, purification, summoning spirits, wind magick. Drink as a tea for an excellent detox and to increase your psychic powers.
  - Root – calling spirits, divination, good luck, protection, wish magick.

  Use either part of the herb for animal protection magick.

- **Geranium:** balancing mind and body, banishing negativity, counteracting love spells, courage, exorcism, fertility, happiness, healing – especially heart healing, mood enhancing, prosperity, protection, resilience, strength, truth.

  Geranium can also treat a host of bowel-related upsets and acts as a natural antiseptic.

- **Gerbera:** energy boost, happiness, love, passion, relieving sorrow.

- **Jasmine:** attractiveness, divination, helping insomnia, new ideas, relaxation, sensuality, sexual healing, wealth and prosperity.

- **Lily:** angels, clearing entities, divine love, fertility, happiness, harmony, helping with legal matters, marriage, prosperity, protection, renewal, safe travel.

- **Marigold:** attracting a new love, cleansing and detoxifying, enhancing current relationships, happiness, healing the skin, inducing prophetic dreams, protection, repelling bugs, swinging things in legal matters, vitality.

- **Rose:** abundance, charms against the evil eye, clearing, healing, love, passion, romance. A tincture of rosewater is soothing for your skin.

  Use pink roses for loyalty and friendship, yellow for peaceful partings, and red for love and lust.

  Use the rosehips (fruit) in healing teas and for emotional healing, luck and spirituality.

Appendix H: Flowers

- **Sunflower:** happiness, health and vitality, potency, power, protection, radiance, strength, truth, wisdom, wish magick. Carries the energy of the Sun.
- **Violet:** calming nerves, creativity, enhancing night magick, gentleness, healing, looking within, peace, prophecy, protection – especially from evil, purity and purification, self-reflection, spirituality, spring.

APPENDIX I
Recommended Resources

Books

Following are a few of my favourite books for both magick and healing:

- *Animal Dreaming,* by Scott Alexander King – an excellent reference guide to help us decipher messages from our animal friends
- *Complete Book of Spells,* by Cassandra Eason
- *Goddess Alive!* and *Goddess Afoot!,* by Michelle Skye
- *The Complete Book of Incense, Oils and Brews,* by Scott Cunningham
- *The Lost Lands,* by Lucy Cavendish
- *Magical Herbalism,* by Scott Cunningham
- *The Secret Language of your Body,* by Inna Segal
- *Wicca: A Guide for the Solitary Practitioner,* by Scott Cunningham
- *The Witches' Goddess* and *The Witches' God,* by Janet and Stewart Farrar
- *Llewellyn's Sabbat Essentials* – there are various authors for these books, so I recommend you look up the series as a whole. It's easy to find on Google.

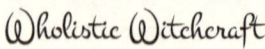

Helpful websites

- Energy Muse – lots of magickal crystal products: www.energymuse.com/
- Lylliths' Emporium – Australian witchcraft supplies: https://lyllithsemporium.com.au/
- The Sacred Willow – Australian Wicca and witchcraft supplies: https://thesacredwillow.com.au/
- Spiritual Healing House – essential oil blends: www.spiritualhealinghouse.com.au/index.html
- The White Witch Parlour – products: www.whitewitchparlour.com/
- The Witchipedia – an online magickal encyclopedia: http://www.witchipedia.com/

Video/audio meditations

- Wiccid Guided Meditation – Journey Through the Chakras: https://wiccid.com.au/shop/wiccid-guided-meditation-chakras/
- Wiccid Guided Meditation – Conversation with Your Higher Self: https://wiccid.com.au/shop/wiccid-guided-meditation-higher-self/
- Wiccid Guided Meditation – Journey to the Underworld for Transformation: https://wiccid.com.au/shop/wiccid-guided-meditation-transformation/

References

Jaynes, J. (2000). *The Origin of Consciousness in the Breakdown of the Bicameral Mind.* Mariner Books (first published 1976 by Houghton Mifflin).

King, S. A. (2007). *Animal Dreaming: The Spiritual and Symbolic Language of the Australasian Animals.* Blue Angel Gallery.

Segal, I. (2007). *The Secret Language of Your Body: The Essential Guide to Health and Wellness.* Blue Angel Gallery.